TRY

ALSO BY DANIEL MacIVOR

TRY

COMMUNION
WAS SPRING
SMALL THINGS
DANIEL MacIVOR

PLAYWRIGHTS CANADA PRESS
TORONTO

For professional or amateur production rights, please contact:
The Gary Goddard Agency
149 Church Street, 2nd Floor
Toronto, ON M5B 1Y4
416-928-0299, meaghan@garygoddardagency.com

LIBRARY AND ARCHIVES CANADA CATALOGUING IN PUBLICATION
MacIvor, Daniel, 1962-
[Plays. Selections]
        Try / Daniel MacIvor. -- First edition.

Collection of three plays.
Contents: Communion -- Was spring -- Small things.
Issued in print and electronic formats.
ISBN 978-1-77091-450-6 (paperback).--ISBN 978-1-77091-451-3 (pdf).--
ISBN 978-1-77091-452-0 (epub).--ISBN 978-1-77091-453-7 (mobi)

        I. MacIvor, Daniel, 1962- Communion. II. MacIvor, Daniel, 1962-Was
spring. III. MacIvor, Daniel, 1962-Small things. IV. Title.

PS8575.I86T79 2015   C812'.54   C2015-904062-0
                                                 C2015-904063-9

We acknowledge the financial support of the Canada Council for the Arts, the Ontario Arts Council (OAC), the Ontario Media Development Corporation and the Government of Canada through the Canada Book Fund for our publishing activities.

 Canada Council for the Arts   Conseil des arts du Canada

 ONTARIO ARTS COUNCIL
CONSEIL DES ARTS DE L'ONTARIO
an Ontario government agency
un organisme du gouvernement de l'Ontario

 Canadä

 Ontario
Ontario Media Development
Corporation

For
Morag MacDonald,
Ellae Elinwood
and
Ashley Gates Jansen

INTRODUCTION
THE THEORETICAL PLAYS

I have never studied playwriting. I wrote my first play when I was an acting student at Dalhousie University in Halifax, Nova Scotia. When I realized as a first-year student that I would not have an opportunity to be on stage until my third year I got together with my equally chagrined classmate, Amy House, and we put on a production of a play called *Blue Bells*. As I remember it I wrote the play and Amy served as a kind of a dramaturge—she may remember it differently. My goals were to get on stage, and to work with Amy, whom I loved and with whom I wanted to perform. We approached our acting teacher John Dunsworth and he agreed to direct us in the play, to be performed for three nights in one of the studios at the theatre school. My pal Sandi Somers agreed to do the lights and set, and Caroline Gillis, my "muse"—according to Kate Taylor of the *Globe and Mail*—was the stage manager. A few months later we took the play to the One Act Play Festival at the University College of Cape Breton and won all the awards (history may remember that differently), including best set—the set was two chairs. It was, in the bubble of whatever world we lived in at that time, a smashing success.

I wrote this play for very specific purposes—to act, for Amy, to work with Sandi and to hang out with Caroline. I knew the space we would be in and we had zero budget and no real resources—hence two chairs. The story itself was nothing too spectacular—I played a thinly veiled version of my father called "He" and Amy played a version of my mother called "She." Structurally the play was two interweaving monologues with one or two moments of dialogue. Thematically it ended up being something about a doomed love. So, *Blue Bells* was my first play and for the purposes of this preface I am going to call it my first Practical Play. A Practical Play is something I define as having clear and specific meta-theatrical, inter-personal and stylistic goals that take the inspirational foreground to story, content and thematic intention.

I went on to write a bunch of other, mostly Practical Plays. These would include the solo performances I created with Daniel Brooks—*House, Here Lies Henry, Monster, Cul-de-sac* and *This Is What Happens Next*—and the multi-character plays I made under the company I ran with Sherrie Johnson, da da kamera, that would include *In On It, You Are Here, The Soldier Dreams* and *A Beautiful View*. My very early work in Toronto in the late '80s and early '90s like *Never Swim Alone, This Is A Play* and *2-2-Tango* I would also call Practical Plays.

In terms of style, anyone who knows me will attest to the fact that I am most comfortable in an environment of minimalism. As Tracy Wright's character says in *A Beautiful View,* "Nothing is sufficient." Minimalism has always appealed to me as a way to engage an audiences' imagination and to honour what I consider the sacred space of the theatre—this is the style I have played with for years—so in that way it is practical in regard to my taste and some sense of my spirit. Also, having toured for years—and before that having had little to no budget—minimalism was economically practical. And then there are the people. First it was Caroline Gillis, certainly not my "muse"—in fact I find this term insulting and verging on misogynistic—but my best friend. Then it was Ed Roy and Ken McDougall—directors and dear friends. Then Daniel Brooks whom I have loved always. Then a series of actors I have written for over the years: Tracy Wright, Darren O'Donnell and later John Beale and Kathryn MacLellan. Then designers, Julie Fox, Andy Moro, Kimberly Purtell.

Wanting to write *for* these people came well before any specific idea of a play. Practically I wanted to be close to these people and explore our personal affection and creative like-mindedness. First would be these people, then "How many voices?" and then "Who?" and then "What does it look like?" "What are the fewest objects I can have on stage?" And then, "What is the stage? How does the stage relate practically—here, now, tonight—to the audience?" And then a theme would emerge. I have never begun a

Practical Play with a theme. In these plays theme has always emerged out of a kind of necessity. And I suppose that's why some people find my work so unsatisfying; there is no one idea or overarching point of view, and the thing that happens is just a thing that happens, it's not the point of the play—usually somebody dies but that's hardly a theme, that's just reality. The point of a Practical Play is the experience of being in a theatre—it's experiential and behavioural and psychological, it's not idea-based. There are ideas contained within, but Practical Plays for me don't start with or revolve exclusively around an idea.

The three plays in *Try* represent what I call my Theoretical Plays. I think of *Try* as a companion piece to *I Still Love You*, the published collection of my five plays made with da da kamera, the Practical Plays. I have had a more varied success with my Theoretical Plays. The first Theoretical Play I wrote, interestingly enough, revisited the story of *Blue Bells* and was called *Somewhere I Have Never Travelled* and it opened the season at Tarragon Theatre in 1988. It was pretty much an unmitigated disaster. I suppose now I can explain why by saying that as I sat to write it my main concern was pleasing the producers for whom I was writing. I had no idea what it should look like or who should be in it (Caroline managed to get a part by auditioning), although I did know what it was about to some extent, and people said it was good writing. And perhaps it was, but good writing it turns out does not make a good play.

Some might consider *Marion Bridge* my next Theoretical Play, although it does not strictly pursue a theme and under any production I've helmed or had influence over it has adhered strictly to my rules of minimalism— nothing on stage that isn't touched by the actor—and the purpose of my writing the play was most practical—to silence my mother as to when I would write a play that she might like. Though it becomes Theoretical due to the fact that it has been restaged so many times and often with cupboards and counters and themes and such.

How It Works, a play I wrote for Mulgrave Road Theatre and that was later produced at Tarragon, also could be thought of as a Theoretical Play—it was the first play I had written that had a door in it—but again I made it in a tiny theatre in Halifax with a group of people I loved and there was no theme to speak of at the outset, and we kept to my rules of minimalism—the door ended up being touched by an actor. Even the very

Theoretical-feeling *Bingo!* had the practicality of trying to make a play that would evoke the style of Norm Foster and might make a ton of money (the money part didn't really work out).

In writing my own history I would consider *Communion* to be my second truly Theoretical Play. The American actress Blythe Danner had seen a production of *Marion Bridge* at a small theatre in New York and got in touch to inquire if I would be interested in writing something that she might perform. I wrote something called *The Communion of Saints* that was rather lumpy and unwieldy and a bit too theoretical and didn't appeal to her. I continued to refine the play and it ended up becoming *Communion*. In a practical sense I had decided after the first draft that I wanted a very particular structure—three dialogues in real time with three actors and each would have a scene with the other—A and B, B and C, C and A—but what makes it a Theoretical play is that I was from the outset pursuing specific themes of communion around therapy and religion and, most centrally, mothering. There was no room for a new theme to emerge from the process of rehearsing the play—that is part of what makes a play Practical. With *Communion* there was a script of ideas to be interpreted.

From *Communion* came the other two plays in the most theoretical sense. I had decided I would write a trilogy of plays that would each involve three women. On a practical level I imagined that the same three actors could do all three but theoretically the plays and their themes existed before the style or the people for the plays. In all three there is a central theme of mothering. In *Was Spring* I wanted to split the mother into three—the mother before, during and after the "event"—and yet to give the sense we were meeting daughters as well. With *Small Things* I wanted to lighten things up a bit, look at these ideas of mothering in a summery way, but with just a bit of gravitas. *Small Things* came out of my time spent working in Stratford—the locals and the city folk not speaking the same emotional language. In each case there was an idea before the play emerged and as a result each play—for better or for worse depending on your personal taste in theatre—is purely about that idea. Each play expands into the theory that created it. A theory that involves themes and ideas and perhaps a notion of what a well-made play is supposed to be. To me it feels I get the most satisfaction, as a maker of theatre, out of the Practical Plays, but those plays don't live as well on paper and are difficult to interpret—it is difficult for most potential directors to see past their minimalism and immediacy. The Theoretical Plays are the plays that are more produced, more seen, and probably the plays that live on.

Maybe if I had studied playwriting I would have been writing theoretically from the beginning, I don't know. But currently I'm getting back into the room of making theatre. Back to the Practical Plays. I'm not sure that I'll write another Theoretical Play. In a sense these three plays represent a period where I tried my best at writing what is considered in the strictest sense a play. In the end I hope you find something here that speaks to you. And if you're a theatre maker maybe there's something practical to be mined from these theoretical plays.

COMMUNION

Communion premiered in a production by Tarragon Theatre in their Mainspace, Toronto, on March 3, 2010, and ran until April 4 with the following cast and creative team:

Carolyn: Sarah Dodd
Leda: Caroline Gillis
Ann: Athena Lamarre

Director: Daniel MacIvor
Dramaturge: Iris Turcott
Set and lighting design: Kimberly Purtell
Costume design: Shawn Kerwin
Sound design: Verne Good

CHARACTERS

Carolyn: a therapist
Leda: a mother
Ann: a daughter

ACT ONE

Music.

In a dim light CAROLYN *and* LEDA *enter and sit facing one another in sleek, modern armchairs. There is a third chair as well, a carpet on the floor. Beside* LEDA *is a small table with a box of tissues on it. The table is hidden from our view.*

CAROLYN *wears an expensive-looking suit, sharp shoes.* LEDA *holds her purse protectively in her lap. She is dressed casually and wears a scarf or a hat on her head, wisps of her short hair are visible.*

A light grows upon CAROLYN, *glowing. She looks out.*

CAROLYN: It's the question. The question you feel in your stomach when it's late and quiet in your room. Alone. When the music has stopped and the television is turned off and the book is closed. The question we fill our days to avoid.

The question that appears loud and unspoken in the eyes of our children, so easily distracted with an ice cream cone. The question in the darkness. And in that darkness there's a door. Look closely and you can see light pouring under the door, through the cracks, at the hinges. A light so bright it might possibly obliterate everything: our rooms, our music, our books, our bodies, our nervous promises to our children and every untouched ice cream cone. The light that will shine on our complicated darkness and expose the simple question we're so afraid to ask. It's not the darkness we fear, it's the light behind the door. It's not the answer we can't hear, it's the question we won't ask.

CAROLYN turns to look at LEDA. *Light shifts. Light up on* CAROLYN *and* LEDA.

CAROLYN, all calmness and focus, watches LEDA *who subtly shifts, sighs, fidgets, groans and grows generally agitated. After some minutes:*

You appear agitated.

LEDA: Jesus. I am agitated.

That took fifteen minutes?

CAROLYN says nothing.

LEDA *looks away as if out a window.*

(sarcastically) "Agitated." Can you not use normal language?

CAROLYN: Can you find another word?

LEDA: This is the face I make when I'm angry.

CAROLYN: Who are you angry with?

LEDA: You mean really or right now?

Silence.

I want to talk. Really I do. But sometimes it's just . . . impossible. Just to imagine talking is impossible. Like climbing a building with my fingers.

Like lifting an elephant. Like mixing concrete with a whisk. Just to start, just to try, it's . . . Sometimes I just can't.

Silence.

Ask me something.

Silence.

"Did you talk to your daughter, Leda?"

Silence.

CAROLYN: Did you talk to Annie?

Silence.

LEDA: Yes.

Silence.

Do you want to know how that went?

Silence.

Waiting waiting waiting. What the hell am I waiting for? My whole life. Waiting for Christmas, waiting for summer, waiting for someone to ask me to dance, waiting to get out of school. That's what drinking was. Waiting for a drink, waiting for the drink to take effect, waiting for another drink. Waiting to die. A life of waiting.

Silence.

Waiting for you to say something.

CAROLYN: What was the effect?

LEDA: The what? Of what?

CAROLYN: Of your drinking?

LEDA: I'm not here to talk about my drinking. I've got my drinking taken care of. I've got my program; I've got my meetings; I've got all that, okay?

Silence.

LEDA sighs.

Silence.

Anyway, okay whatever what? What were you going to say?

CAROLYN: You said you would wait for the drink. You would wait for the drink to take effect. You would wait for another drink. But what about the effect?

LEDA: What about it?

CAROLYN: What was the effect?

LEDA: I got drunk. Jesus.

CAROLYN: I'm curious—

LEDA: You're curious? That's good. That's a sign of life.

Pause.

Sorry.

CAROLYN: I'm curious about a relationship between this "waiting" and this "effect."

LEDA: What?

CAROLYN: Perhaps in the "effect" this feeling of waiting went away.

LEDA looks at CAROLYN for a few moments.

LEDA: So what? I should start drinking again? Thanks.

Silence.

Sorry I know you're not saying that. I'm just pissy today.

CAROLYN: You're pissy today.

LEDA looks away, as if out a window.

LEDA: Yeah. I don't know why. This fucking weather.

Silence.

You know when I talk to people about you I call you Carolyn. I don't say "my therapist," I say "Carolyn."

Silence.

Like you're my friend. It's not like you're my friend. "Carolyn says." "I saw Carolyn today." Like you're a friend or something. And you're not. It's not like I can say . . . Like those shoes. Can you walk in those shoes? Do you have a pair of running shoes stashed somewhere that you wear home? Which I would ask a friend. But instead I just think about it. You walking home in your running shoes and passing people and them not realizing you're this person all full of other people's shit and secrets.

Them thinking you're just some secretary. Like poor old Margaret out there.

CAROLYN: Margo.

LEDA: I know, I know, I just call her Margaret because she still calls me "Linda." How many times do I have to tell her: "Leda." After three months of "Linda" she's Margaret to me now . . . Or is it four months? What is it, February?

Silence.

But get my name right, come on! Although it's kinda hilarious.

CAROLYN: Why is it hilarious?

Silence.

LEDA: I think she's smoking out there. Sometimes I come in I can smell it. I mean come on why can't I smoke in here? Of all the places a person should be able to smoke it should be here. How am I supposed to be able to think? Especially if she's out there sneaking them. I know she smokes.

Pause.

I mean I don't know for sure she smokes *out there*—I don't have any hard evidence I mean, but I know she's a smoker. Those little lines around the lips.

Pause.

That's what got to me really, what it does to your skin. I've only ever tried to quit out of vanity. I never tried that hard though. After I quit the booze it was all I had left. That and the coffee. And the sugar. And the bad television. I was up till after four the other night watching the Shopping Channel. As long as I don't start buying shit. I can get addicted to anything.

Silence. LEDA *looks away as if out a window.*

Is it raining every time I come here? Is it raining every Wednesday? I don't mind rain normally. Spring rain or summer rain. I don't mind snow. But this winter rain is evil.

Silence.

Jesus I'm not here to talk about the weather. Not at these prices.

Silence.

CAROLYN: Have you had that dream again?

LEDA groans.

Silence.

LEDA: Which one?

CAROLYN: The dream with the door.

LEDA: Yeah, I always have that dream.

CAROLYN: Is there anything different about it?

LEDA: No.

Silence.

Yeah, actually yeah. Now in the dream I'm wondering what the dream means, which maybe means I'm seeing you too much.

CAROLYN: You're aware that you're dreaming in the dream?

LEDA: Yeah. No. I don't know.

CAROLYN: Is the other woman still there?

LEDA: There's more than one woman, maybe you should take notes.

CAROLYN: How many women are there?

LEDA: I don't know, two or three, two.

CAROLYN: And what are the two women doing?

LEDA: Watching me. Waiting.

CAROLYN: Waiting.

LEDA: That's what I said.

CAROLYN: What do you imagine they're waiting for?

LEDA: I don't know.

(sardonically) Maybe it's a bathroom. Maybe it's a lineup.

CAROLYN: Have you tried what we talked about?

LEDA: To open the door?

CAROLYN: Yes.

LEDA: No.

    Pause.

Why bother, I know what's behind the door.

CAROLYN: What's behind the door?

LEDA: Probably you know, total destruction. The end of the world. Black skies, tribes of zombie cannibals wearing Mardi Gras beads, smoking volcanoes, smouldering carcasses of cars. The regular stuff.

    LEDA looks away, as if out a window.

Rain. Burning rain.

Silence.

CAROLYN: Can you change what you imagine behind the door?

LEDA: In the dream?

CAROLYN: Or now.

LEDA closes her eyes a moment. She feigns concentration. She opens her eyes.

LEDA: Nope.

Silence.

God! How can you stand me! I am so predictable. I'm just another patient!

(to herself) Get over it get over it get over it. Fuck. You know—you remember that week I came in here—and we never talked about this and I kept waiting for you to say something, which really pissed me off actually that you didn't. But that week I came in and I sat in that chair instead of this chair? Which you probably don't remember but fuck it. Anyway. And why I did it was because I always sat in this chair and I decided—and I really thought about this—but I decided I was going to come in—and I was even—I was even thinking about it the week before. While I was sitting here in this chair that I always sit in, I was thinking that next week I was going to come in and sit in that chair. Because if I did—if I changed chairs, that would show I was the kind of person who would all of a sudden— after a month or whatever in a chair—the kind of person who didn't get attached to a particular chair—that I was unpredictable. That I was not like everyone else—I was special. But what's so sad—so pathetic—I walk in the office and you're all standing by the door like you always are, and I'm all heading for the new unpredictable chair, and I think "what if I sat

in her chair"—your chair—the chair you always sit in. But I don't, because I've already got my plan to sit in the new unpredictable chair. Which is not unpredictable at all because now I'm just following my plan. How predictable is that? You can't plan to be unpredictable. I just wanted to *appear* unpredictable. I want you to *think* I'm unpredictable. And why do I care what you think? And you know why I care what you think?

Because I have no idea what you think. If you think. I mean I'm sure you do, I'm sure they train you to think without showing you're thinking. But are you even thinking about me? Are you just thinking about what the book says? Whatever the book is, there's some book I'm sure. Some book that talks about all the other fuck-ups like me who come in here and talk about their dreams and their daughters and their pointless fear of death and their relationships. And thank God I'm not dating, thankfully that's not an option—being in here wasting all this time and money talking about some fucking man. And don't repeat that back to me that I said "some fucking man." It's not—it's nothing—I'm not going to talk about men. I'm done with that. But you're like some kind of—some kind of—cyborg or something. Some kind of— Because I look at you all calm and focused and I keep hoping that really you're crawling the walls inside yourself screaming "Shut up! Shut up! Shut up!" Like—like—like the rest of us. Like you have feelings. Like somewhere in here you've got a pair of secret running shoes stashed that you walk home in. I mean not that—of course you don't walk home—I don't imagine you even take public transit. But just that you have running shoes somewhere in the world somewhere.

Silence.

CAROLYN: Running shoes.

LEDA groans.

Would my having running shoes make me predictable or unpredictable?

LEDA: Oh my God! I don't know. Predictable.

CAROLYN: You'd like me to be predictable.

LEDA: I guess so!

CAROLYN: But you'd like to be unpredictable.

LEDA: I don't— I'm not— Fine fine. I want to be unpredictable. There, okay? Great. A breakthrough.

CAROLYN: And to be unpredictable is to be?

LEDA: Not predictable.

CAROLYN: Which is?

LEDA: I don't know. Less . . . More . . . Different.

CAROLYN: Different than?

LEDA groans.

Silence.

LEDA: Everyone . . . else. And I'm not.

Fine. I just . . . I know.

Silence.

LEDA sighs.

Silence.

She's back at her father's. That's where I tracked her down. She was distant. This civil distance. Serene.

Playing at serene. It's not serene it's . . . What's that word you like so much? . . . Evasive. Evasive dressed up as serene. It's all so loaded. I was going to talk to her about coming up to see her. But I didn't. What am I supposed to say? She was fine, everything was fine. "Fine. Fine. Very good. Thank you. Fine. God bless." "God bless." And Annie knows how that . . . She just does it to get to me.

CAROLYN: Annie does it to get to you.

LEDA: Yeah yeah. I'm so special. It's all about me.

Silence.

I spoke to Stephanie. She answered when I called the house. Doug won't even pick up the phone if he sees that it's me. Damn call display. Usually I can get some information from Stephanie but she was weirder than usual. She's always weird but weirder than usual. Sort of babbling. She's opening a spa. And apparently Doug's all for it. Which I can't believe considering Doug and money. A spa? Up there? Who can afford a spa, their main industry is Walmart. Poor Stephanie. I have a soft spot for Stephanie. Not always. At first I was . . . I don't know . . . threatened I guess. Like when Annie was sixteen and she told me she didn't want to call me "Mom" anymore. At first I thought it was because of Stephanie. So I said, "What do you call Stephanie?" I was thinking, you know, that Stephanie was more of a mother to her or something. And so I said to Annie, "What do you call Stephanie?" And she said "Moron."

LEDA laughs.

Poor Stephanie.

Silence.

I miss that.

CAROLYN: You miss?

LEDA: That Annie. The cutting . . . funny . . . The sarcasm.

CAROLYN: You never mentioned that Annie doesn't call you "Mom."

LEDA: Ancient history.

CAROLYN: How do you feel about that?

LEDA: I dealt with it.

CAROLYN: How?

LEDA: By dealing with it. Anyway it's no big deal. What's in a name? Don't tell Margo I said that.

Silence.

CAROLYN: You said you missed that Annie.

LEDA: "That Annie"?

CAROLYN: That sarcastic Annie. Who is this Annie?

LEDA: I don't know.

Silence.

God. I never thought I'd be nostalgic for the days when she used to run around with drug dealers and get into fist fights at school. I thought she was going to end up being a lesbian. She always seemed like a lesbian to me. I would have rathered that. I even encouraged it.

Silence.

I saw your picture in that gay paper with your girlfriend. Or partner or whatever. She's a cutie. And I'm not saying you should have told me or anything. It's not an issue. I don't care. I like lesbians.

CAROLYN: Do you like Annie?

LEDA: Do I like my daughter? That's a stupid question.

Silence.

Why would you even ask that?

Silence.

Yeah yeah yeah.

Silence.

Her religion stuff is just so . . . This "Fellowship of Christ the King Your Righteous Avenging Soldier of Fetuses" or whatever it is—I mean she can love Jesus Christ, I have no problem with that. I'm sure he was a lovely guy; he would have made a great roommate. He'd be one of those perfect dinner-party guests who tells good stories and knows how to pass the talking stick. And if we were having dinner and he passed the talking stick to me I'd probably even give him my turn. She can have her religion, I just don't want her to sell it to me. Leave me out of it.

CAROLYN: Sell it to you.

LEDA: What?

CAROLYN: Sell it to you.

LEDA: Yeah, what?

CAROLYN: You said—

LEDA: I know what I said. Why don't I just talk to a tape recorder and play it back? I could do it at home. It'd be cheaper. And I could smoke.

Silence.

Okay so what? "Sell it to me." Fine okay. And I'm not buying. Is that what you're getting at? Shouldn't I want to buy something my daughter's selling? If she was selling Girl Guide cookies I'd buy a dozen. So she's selling something and I'm not buying and so I feel guilty. There. Is that the . . . I don't know . . . What?

CAROLYN: But she's not selling Girl Guide cookies.

LEDA: *(exasperatedly)* Oh my God.

CAROLYN: What is she selling?

Silence.

LEDA: I used to go to church. I liked going to mass. But when I went it was all guys in beards and sandals with guitars singing Carole King songs. But now it's all gotten so serious. At least the lot she's gotten hooked up with are. I don't remember it being so serious. Jail? I mean— And she went happily. Like going to jail was the prize for burning down the abortion clinic. I mean she made her point. She never had a problem making a point. But arson is arson. In court she was all serenity. Smiles and serenity. But I think the reality wasn't so sunny. She hasn't said anything to me about it since she got out, but I get the feeling she's in no big hurry to go back. I don't know. It's so extreme. At least she believes in something, I guess. Or maybe . . . Sometimes I just think . . .

Pause.

CAROLYN: Sometimes you think . . .

Silence.

LEDA: That I'm so special. I know, I know.

Silence.

CAROLYN: You said you liked to go to mass.

LEDA: Yeah, when I was a kid.

CAROLYN: Why?

LEDA: Getting dressed up. It was social. Boys.

Pause.

You'd get a new outfit and you'd wear it on Sunday because you'd get to do the whole parade to communion thing. Up the aisle, across the front, back up the aisle. Everybody checking everybody out. The Catholic fashion runway. Or maybe it was just me. Maybe everybody else was . . . I was always watching people coming from communion. You were supposed to be praying but . . . and this is back in the day when the priest would put the host thing right on your tongue. Like it was so holy you weren't allowed to touch it . . . Everybody would look different after. They'd get their communion and then as they were walking away they looked . . . different. Peaceful. Holy. Like something touched them. Or they felt something. They knew . . . something. They got it. I never did. I never felt anything. I didn't get it. You know?

CAROLYN: Yes.

LEDA: "Yes"?

CAROLYN says nothing.

You just said "yes."

CAROLYN says nothing.

Did you just agree with me? Was that a slip?

CAROLYN says nothing.

You want to talk about it? We could go for coffee. You could wear your running shoes.

CAROLYN says nothing.

Joke! Man, you're a tough audience.

CAROLYN: I'm not your audience, Leda.

LEDA groans.

LEDA looks at her watch. She sighs. Silence.

Does Annie get it?

LEDA: What? My jokes?

CAROLYN: This "something."

LEDA: This what? God, I need an interpreter with you.

CAROLYN: You said that people looked different after they took communion. Like they got something. Does Annie get it?

LEDA: I guess. She must. Or she thinks she does.

CAROLYN: She thinks she does.

LEDA: "*Or* she thinks she does." Or she must. She must. I guess she must.

CAROLYN: What if she doesn't? What would that mean?

LEDA: It would mean . . . I don't know. Maybe you should talk to her.

Silence.

I didn't buy that wig. Remember I said I was looking at that wig? I didn't buy it.

Silence.

Some people after the chemo it doesn't grow back at all. So I guess I'm lucky. But it's so short. I look terrible with short hair. What difference does it make now though. I would have stayed bald if it meant getting rid of it.

What a waste of time. I mean there were no guarantees it would take, right?

Silence.

Annie's never seen me with short hair. She wouldn't care. If I saw her. I mean I will see her. It's getting ridiculous. It's been over six months. It's not like she's . . . I mean it's just a couple of hours on the train. More like three. The better part of three. But it's also . . .

Like going home for me. Which is loaded. You know?

Silence.

At some point I'm going to have to see her. To tell her. I'm not going to tell her on the phone. Sooner or later I'm going to have to see her. Sooner really. She'll know something's up if my hair's this short. Maybe I should buy the wig. I mean it's not like she'll care.

CAROLYN: It's not like she'll care.

LEDA: What I look like.

CAROLYN: Why wouldn't she care what you looked like?

LEDA: Because she only cares about my soul. That's all that matters about anybody, their fucking soul.

CAROLYN: And how does that make you feel?

LEDA: Safe in the arms of Jesus.

CAROLYN: That's how it makes you feel?

LEDA: Are you wearing a sarcasm filter today?

CAROLYN: Sarcasm isn't a feeling.

> *LEDA groans.*

Can you give me a feeling?

LEDA: Pissed off.

CAROLYN: Who are you pissed off at?

LEDA: Besides you?

> *LEDA sighs. She looks away as if out a window. She considers CAROLYN's question. She disappears into her thoughts a moment. She pulls herself back.*

Well it's not "God" or something. I'm not angry at "God." How could I be angry at "God"? I don't believe in "God."

What? Some old bearded son of a bitch on a throne with a sceptre who hates fags and loves fetuses? Please. Some entity I'm supposed to suffer for and praise? Who will punish me? I've got that covered.

> *Silence.*

I'm not saying I don't believe in anything. I've got my own Higher Power thing, it's all good. It's personal.

Someone once said at a meeting that "God" is just "good" with a letter missing. I can get my head around that kinda stuff. Something uncomplicated. I'm complicated enough.

CAROLYN: Complicated.

LEDA: What?

CAROLYN: Is complicated more like predictable or more like unpredictable?

LEDA: What?

CAROLYN: Is being complicated more like being—

LEDA: No, I mean why? What does that have to do with anything?

CAROLYN: Earlier you said—

LEDA: No I know. What, I've got the memory of a goldfish? I mean what does one have to do with the other. That drives me crazy. It's this loop-de-loop thing you do when the session's running down. You make some connection to something I said before so that it feels like we're making some progress or something. And I'm supposed to go home and think about that or some fucking thing.

CAROLYN: Leda—

LEDA: Yes Mom?

CAROLYN: Mom?

LEDA: That "Leda" had a Mom tone. Like I was going to get a "Mom" talking to. Like what was going to come after it was "Leda, if you don't clean your room you'll never find your socks" . . . or whatever. Which isn't bad advice if your room is messy and your feet are cold. Some advice, that would be nice.

CAROLYN: Like a mother would give.

LEDA: What?

CAROLYN: Advice like a mother might give.

LEDA: And you're not my mother. I know. Gee, is that the best you can do? Where did you study, the city college?

CAROLYN: I need you to stop being evasive.

LEDA: I need you to give me some actual advice.

CAROLYN: Leda, would you like to re-evaluate our continuing to work together?

LEDA: No. Christ. Every time I ask for something specific you want to break up.

CAROLYN: To break up.

LEDA looks at CAROLYN for a few moments.

LEDA: Honest to God, you say things and I don't know if you're asking me something or trying to tell me something.

You know what a question mark is? People use it at the end of a sentence. It makes your voice go up so the other person knows if you're asking or telling. Or am I just stupid? Fuck.

LEDA starts to become overwhelmed and begins to search through her purse for a tissue.

Jesus, you never have any tissue.

Not finding a tissue in her purse she becomes increasingly frustrated.

Just give me some advice. Just tell me what to do. Say "go see Annie." Why do you never even say that? I have to do it all by myself? I'm so on my own here. I'm so on my fucking own. Why do you never have tissues!

LEDA throws her purse on the floor and its contents scatter. CAROLYN sits forward as if to help, then stops herself.

I'm sorry I'm sorry I'm sorry I'm sorry.

LEDA gets on her knees, gathering her things from the floor; she is crying now.

I'm terrible at everything. I'm a terrible patient, I'm a terrible mother, I was a terrible drunk, I'm terrible at living, I'm terrible at dying.

CAROLYN: What's under your anger? Leda?

LEDA: What?

CAROLYN: What's under your anger?

LEDA: I'm not . . . I don't know. I'm pissed off.

CAROLYN: What's under the feeling of anger?

LEDA: Under it? Nothing. Me. More anger.

CAROLYN: *(to snap LEDA out of it)* You're special.

LEDA: What?

CAROLYN: Are you afraid?

A moment as LEDA *looks at* CAROLYN.

LEDA: I just want a tissue.

CAROLYN: There are tissues behind you.

LEDA *looks around.*

On the table beside your chair.

LEDA *sits. She takes some tissues from the table.*

Silence.

LEDA: I don't know what I feel. That's why I'm here.

CAROLYN: I can't tell you how you feel.

LEDA: Then what can you do?

Silence.

CAROLYN: If you weren't talking to me who would you be talking to?

LEDA: I am talking to you.

CAROLYN: I can't—

LEDA: Neither can I.

Silence.

LEDA *looks away as if out a window. She becomes calm.*

Has that table always been there?

CAROLYN: Yes.

LEDA: I never noticed it before.

CAROLYN: It's a low table.

LEDA: It is. It's little.

LEDA looks at her watch.

CAROLYN: If it makes a difference . . . I do have running shoes.

Silence.

LEDA: I'm over. Sorry I went over.

LEDA gathers her things to leave.

CAROLYN: Do you need a moment?

LEDA: No. I'm good.

LEDA rises. CAROLYN rises. LEDA moves to leave.

CAROLYN: Leda?

LEDA stops.

Go see Annie.

Light fades. In the dim light CAROLYN and LEDA exit.

Music.

ACT TWO

Music continues.

In the dim light ANN *enters. A generic hotel room. A bed, chairs, a night table, a telephone; off, a bathroom.*

ANN *is sturdy and blunt. She wears a parka and a hat. Under the parka she is wearing a cotton dress with a delicate pattern.*

A light grows upon ANN, *glowing. She prays in a gentle, private way.*

ANN: Father, in light of the work of Jesus for me, concerning all of these whom You want to convert, and whom You want to bring to grace: forgive them their sins and misdeeds, since they do not yet know what they are doing. Do not hold this against them for our sakes, but convert them and us together, according to Your holy will, as soon as it may please You. We ask this for the sake of Your holy name. Lord, you are my owner, help me to remember that Jesus has purchased me with His blood, and now I do not belong to myself, but to You. I am Yours. Amen and amen and hallelujah.

ANN turns and looks at the room. Light shifts. Light up on the hotel room.

ANN looks around the room. She does not remove her hat or parka.

LEDA: *(off)* Have a seat hon, I'll just be a sec.

ANN: Okay.

LEDA: *(off)* Is it cold out?

ANN: It's okay.

LEDA: *(off)* I'll just be a sec.

ANN: This is an expensive hotel.

LEDA: *(off)* How's Stephanie?

ANN: Fine.

LEDA: *(off)* How's the spa?

ANN: The what?

LEDA: *(off)* Stephanie's spa.

ANN: I don't know.

LEDA: *(off)* Are you kidding me? That's all she talks about whenever I call.

ANN: She always has a plan for something.

LEDA: *(off)* How's your father?

ANN: Fine.

> *LEDA enters from the bathroom. She is casually dressed though it's clear she has made some effort. She holds one earlobe.*

LEDA: Hi, sweetie. I think I dropped an earring over here.

LEDA looks on the floor near the bed for her earring.

ANN: Hi.

LEDA: I got them in Florida last year. Oh there you are, you bugger.

LEDA picks up the earring and moves to return to the bathroom to put it in.

Look at that bedspread, isn't that ugly? You're all bundled up, is it that cold?

ANN: It's not cold if you're bundled up.

LEDA: Well it's nice and cozy in here, take off your coat.

ANN sits on the bed. She pulls off her hat but does not open her parka.

ANN: Your hair's different.

LEDA: Yeah. What are you wearing?

ANN: A parka.

LEDA: No I mean you're wearing a dress. Are you going somewhere? I thought we'd just hang out here, or go for a walk or some soup.

ANN: There's a muffin place close.

LEDA: Oh. Okay. Is it formal?

ANN: This is how I always dress now.

LEDA: Oh. This is a new thing?

ANN: It's a deeper commitment.

LEDA: To? . . .

ANN: We wear what the redeemed shall wear.

LEDA: Oh. Right. Okay. I should be fine then.

LEDA exits to the bathroom.

(*off*) So how do you know?

ANN: Know what?

LEDA: (*off*) What the redeemed shall wear? Who tells you?

ANN: It's in the Bible.

LEDA: (*off*) Oh yeah? I didn't know there was a fashion section.

ANN: It's not something to laugh at.

LEDA: (*off*) No.

ANN: This is an expensive hotel.

LEDA: (*off*) It's just a hotel.

ANN: You could have stayed at Dad's.

LEDA: (*off*) Yeah right.

ANN: He doesn't care.

LEDA: (*off*) Yes he does.

ANN: Stephanie doesn't care.

LEDA: (*off*) How's all that working out?

ANN: All what?

LEDA enters from the bathroom.

LEDA: You living there with your father and Stephanie?

ANN: I'm not there anymore.

LEDA: Where are you?

ANN: Bud's.

LEDA: Who's Bud?

ANN: I got married.

LEDA: What?

ANN: I got married.

LEDA: You got married?

ANN: Yup.

LEDA: When?

ANN: It was a small thing at the church.

LEDA: Who did you marry?

ANN: Bud.

LEDA: Who's Bud?

ANN: He's downstairs.

LEDA: You're like a stealth bomber. You should be classified with the military. Why didn't you tell me? Does your father know?

ANN: Yeah of course. He was there.

LEDA: Was Stephanie there?

ANN: I couldn't not invite Stephanie.

LEDA: But you could not invite me?

ANN: I didn't think you'd care.

LEDA: I wouldn't care?

ANN: I was waiting to tell you in person and you kept saying you were coming up and then cancelling at the last minute.

LEDA: You couldn't have come to see me to tell me?

ANN: I'm telling you now.

LEDA: When did this happen?

ANN: August.

LEDA: August? That's six months ago.

ANN: Seven.

LEDA: I saw you in July. You must have known then. Why didn't you talk to me about it then?

ANN: We didn't talk we fought.

LEDA: And no one told me. Your father didn't tell me.

ANN: Dad understood why I didn't want to.

LEDA: Oh he did?

ANN: He knows you. Stephanie wanted to but she knew my wishes.

LEDA: You could— Your wishes? What are your wishes?

ANN: I don't want to fight about it.

LEDA: You could have . . .

No wonder Stephanie's been so weird on the phone.

ANN: She knew I was waiting to tell you in person.

LEDA: How long have you known Bud?

ANN: I knew him before.

LEDA: Before what?

ANN: Before I went to jail. He works for the Fellowship.

LEDA: The Fellowship?

ANN: Yes.

LEDA: In what capacity? Recruiter?

ANN: He takes care of the buildings and the grounds.

Silence.

What? What?

LEDA: Nothing.

ANN: What?

LEDA: Why would you do this without telling me?

ANN: You didn't tell me every time you went on a two-week bender.

LEDA: It's not the same.

ANN: I'm telling you now.

LEDA: So you up and fell in love with a janitor and married him?

ANN: He's not just a janitor. And what difference does it make if he was a janitor? People don't marry people because of their jobs.

LEDA: People don't get married without telling their mother.

ANN: People don't have mothers like you.

> *Silence.*

LEDA: Does he make a decent living?

ANN: It's a good job.

LEDA: Good how?

ANN: Good enough. And he does some ministry.

LEDA: Oh my God he is a recruiter.

ANN: He has a powerful message. He's touched by the Grace of God.

LEDA: Was this some kind of arranged marriage or something? Through the Fellowship?

ANN: No.

LEDA: God, give me the Catholics any day over this lot.

They're so *right*. In every way. Everything's not black and white.

ANN: Yes it is.

LEDA: Well that argument's over.

ANN: I'm not arguing. I'm telling you what I believe.

LEDA: You're married?

ANN: Yes.

LEDA: And Stephanie was there?

ANN: Stephanie was only there because Dad was there and Dad was only there because he paid for the wedding.

LEDA: Your father paid for the wedding?

ANN: Yeah.

LEDA: Oh yeah, Bud's got a good job.

ANN: That's what fathers do.

LEDA: And mothers are supposed to buy flowers and things. You could have given me that chance. To help pick out the wedding dress. I didn't even get to see you in your wedding dress. That's not fair.

ANN: And it's not fair to decide you want to be a mother now when you never were before.

Silence.

Are you still not drinking?

LEDA: I haven't had a drink in two years, Annie.

ANN: You've gone that long before.

LEDA: No I haven't actually, not since before you were born.

Silence.

Take your coat off for God's sake.

ANN: Let's go out. Bud's waiting to meet us in the lobby. The muffin place is just around the corner.

LEDA: This is a full-out ambush. You used to do this when you were a kid, hiding behind corners and in closets and leaping out at me.

ANN: It's not about you.

LEDA: He's a janitor?

ANN: Jesus was a carpenter.

LEDA: But he didn't make a living at it, did he? Does this one actually think he's Jesus?

ANN: Lawrence was fine until he started seeing that head doctor.

LEDA: Uh-huh.

ANN: What?

LEDA: Oh Annie. You don't actually believe that?

ANN: You only met Lawrence once that Christmas at Gramma's.

LEDA: Stephanie told me the stories. It was Lawrence who started all this.

ANN: All this what?

LEDA: Lawrence was as crazy as a bag of wet cats.

ANN: No he wasn't. Not at first.

LEDA: At Christmas dinner he told Gramma she was going to die.

ANN: And she did.

LEDA: She was ninety-five. It was inappropriate.

ANN: But when he started talking to that head doctor he got so much worse. He started talking to that head doctor when he should have been talking to God.

LEDA: Oh Annie.

ANN: It was the conversation he should have been having with God. Head doctors think they're God.

Pause.

LEDA: I was seeing a head doctor.

ANN: What? Why?

LEDA: To work through some things.

ANN: Are you not going to those meetings anymore?

LEDA: No I am still going to "those meetings."

ANN: Where they tell you that God is a tree or something.

LEDA: Anything that isn't me.

ANN: A coffee cup or something.

LEDA: Can we not get into God?

ANN: It's your soul.

How could you afford a head doctor?

LEDA: It's amazing how much money you save when you stop buying wine by the case.

ANN: So you're not going to the head doctor anymore?

LEDA: I got what I needed.

ANN: He gave you pills?

LEDA: She. Carolyn. No. I don't take pills.

ANN: A woman doctor?

LEDA: Yes.

ANN: Women shouldn't be doctors.

LEDA: Oh really?

ANN: Women should raise their children and obey their husbands.

LEDA: Do the redeemed also live in the Middle Ages?

ANN: The redeemed obey the word of God.

LEDA: And their husbands.

ANN: If this woman's husband lets her be a doctor then he's not redeemed, so no, he shouldn't be obeyed.

LEDA: Well Carolyn's a lesbian and there's no husband to "let her" or to obey, so I guess it wouldn't be an issue for her.

> *Pause.*

I'm assuming that in the Middle Ages lesbians aren't redeemed? Or maybe there are no lesbians in the Middle Ages?

> *Pause.*

ANN: I pray for you. I really do.

> *Silence.*

LEDA: What kind of a name is "Bud"?

ANN: His real name is Brian but everyone calls him Bud.

LEDA: Does he drive a truck?

ANN: Why?

LEDA: You like them with trucks. Lawrence had a truck, didn't he? And there was that drug dealer in high school.

ANN: I was the drug dealer, he just drove me around.

LEDA: You were the drug dealer?

ANN: Yeah.

LEDA: *(wistfully)* Those were the days. What does Stephanie think of Bud?

ANN: Stephanie only thinks about Stephanie.

LEDA *laughs.*

But she is making us dinner tonight.

LEDA: *(suddenly serious)* Dinner with Stephanie?

ANN: Yeah.

LEDA: I have to laugh. It doesn't matter but I just have to laugh. Stephanie's at the wedding and I don't even know it's happening. Stephanie gets dinner and I get muffins. Boy oh boy am I down on the list.

ANN: You're coming too. Dinner for all of us, we're all going to dinner at Dad's.

LEDA: Well I'm not sure I want to have dinner with your father not speaking to me and Stephanie blathering.

ANN: I don't want to do it either.

LEDA: Why didn't you invite me to your wedding?

ANN: You wouldn't have come.

LEDA: Yes I would have.

ANN: Or you would have come but not really wanted to, or you would have complained about it. You would have turned it into all about you.

Pause.

LEDA: Okay. We'll deal with this later or . . . Well there's nothing to deal with now it's done.

ANN: Let's go.

LEDA: I need some time alone with you.

ANN: Bud's waiting in the lobby.

LEDA: Just call the desk and tell him to wait in the bar.

ANN: In the bar?

LEDA: Or we'll meet him at the muffin place. I need some time with you now.

ANN: Are you really not drinking?

LEDA: No, for God's sake; do you want a urine sample?

ANN goes to the phone.

ANN: Okay fine. But I am going to call though. Because he's already been waiting.

LEDA: Yes fine.

ANN: *(on the phone to the front desk)* Hello, do you see a big man in a cowboy hat and a beard sitting by the front door? . . . Could you tell him that Ann said we'd meet him in a little while at the muffin place?

. . . Yes that place . . . Right on. Thanks. God bless.

ANN hangs up.

She says the muffin place is nice.

LEDA: You're "Ann" now.

ANN: Yes.

LEDA: I see.

ANN: People change their names.

LEDA: Yes they do. But usually it's because they didn't like who they were before.

ANN: It doesn't matter who I was before. I'm Ann now.

LEDA: What was wrong with "Annie"?

LEDA laughs.

Where did Annie go? What did you do with Annie?

ANN: It has nothing to do with you.

Silence.

LEDA: "Ann and Bud"?

ANN: Yup.

LEDA: I just worry that you go for the crazy ones. And I understand that, your father was a little crazy when I met him, well he's still crazy but Stephanie seems to balance him out.

ANN: "Crazy"?

LEDA: We're all a little crazy.

ANN: Do you think you're crazy? Is that why you were seeing a head doctor?

LEDA: No. That's not why.

Silence.

I was . . . Trying to find some peace of mind.

ANN: I guess it didn't work. You don't look very happy.

LEDA: Misery bonds us.

ANN: What?

LEDA: Remember? "Misery bonds us."

ANN: That was a long time ago.

LEDA: "Misery bonds us.
In a hurricane of tears
We find Spring showers."

What was that? Thirteen? Grade eight?

ANN: Something like that.

LEDA: You were always so deep, dark even, but sensitive. Sensitive but you wouldn't take anything from anyone.

ANN: I took anything from you.

LEDA: You took care of me. And I know I shouldn't have put you in that position. But maybe though, a little maybe it helped you to be strong. You're a very strong young woman. You know when you got arrested I was kind of proud of you. For standing up for what you believe in.

ANN: I thought you were pro-abortion.

LEDA: It's called pro-choice.

ANN: Well I wasn't proud of me. We should have burned the place down with all those killers inside.

LEDA: Annie, don't say that.

ANN: And I might some time.

LEDA: You can't think like that and call yourself a Christian.

ANN: Yes I can. And I can with peace in my soul.

LEDA: If I had that kind of peace I'd be looking for the antidote.

ANN: Well you don't have to worry about it. I know the Truth. You don't want it that's fine.

LEDA: There are many truths.

ANN: So the liars will have us believe.

LEDA: You're at peace?

ANN: Yes.

LEDA: This is peace?

ANN: Yes.

LEDA: Then why does it feel so angry?

ANN: That's you.

LEDA: You're afraid.

ANN: That's you. You think you're seeing me but you're only seeing yourself.

LEDA: Maybe. Maybe.

ANN: Are you going to come and meet Bud or not?

LEDA: I will okay, in a minute. I will. But. There will be no talk of the Fellowship or Living the Truth or my soul.

ANN: Bud has a powerful message.

LEDA: I don't want to listen to it today.

ANN: Maybe you should listen for once.

LEDA: You're telling me to listen? When have you ever listened? Other than to Lawrence who thought he was Jesus and to Bud who you apparently think is God.

ANN: Maybe you should listen before it's too late.

LEDA: It's too late. I'm not interested in having my soul saved. My soul is fine. It's mine, it's fine, I'll be good with whatever. Leave it be. Really. Promise me. If you love me.

ANN: Promise you?

LEDA: Promise me that from now on it will just be one of those things we don't talk about. If you love me. Do you love me?

ANN: What?

LEDA: Do you love me?

ANN: Love the sinner, hate the sin.

LEDA: I'm not talking about an idea. I'm not talking about scripture. I'm asking if you love me, Annie. Me. I don't want you to love my soul; I want you to love me.

ANN: You are your soul.

LEDA: Me Annie. Me.

ANN: Me me me.

LEDA: Please Annie. This isn't easy.

> *ANN takes off her coat. She cradles her belly. We see that she is pregnant. She stands facing LEDA.*

ANN: I wanted Bud to be here for this.

LEDA: For what? Oh God.

> *LEDA sits.*

ANN: It's a beautiful thing. It's what I was meant to do.

LEDA: How pregnant are you?

ANN: Six months.

LEDA: You didn't waste any time.

ANN: It's what I was meant to do.

LEDA: Oh God . . .

ANN: You're not happy?

LEDA: No I'm just . . . I'm . . . It's the timing.

ANN: Does it make you feel old or something?

LEDA: No no, I'm happy. If you're happy I'm happy for you.

ANN: You don't seem happy.

LEDA: Sit down, I want to talk to you.

ANN: We'll go and see Bud now.

LEDA: Sit down.

Silence.

Does Bud love you?

ANN: Does he love me?

LEDA: Yes.

ANN: Yes he does. More than anyone ever has.

Silence.

LEDA: I have this dream—

ANN: A dream?

LEDA: Annie. Please. For five minutes? For your mother?

Silence.

I have this dream. I'm in a dark room with other people, women, watching me, and I'm standing in front of a door. And I'm standing there expecting the door to open. Like it should just open by itself. But it doesn't. And I'm standing there and I can't move and I'm looking at the door and I'm not sure if I'm hoping it opens or hoping it doesn't open. Carolyn told me to open the door. Just open it. And that sounds easy but . . . At first I thought the dream had something to do with death. But now I don't think so. I think it has something to do with fear.

ANN: Why are you telling me this?

LEDA: I don't want you to be so afraid.

ANN: I'm not afraid.

LEDA: Why don't I believe you?

ANN: Why are you telling me this?

LEDA: I don't want drama, Annie. This is just information I need to impart. And the timing couldn't be worse I guess. Or I don't know maybe it couldn't be better. But I want you to know I'm good with this. I'm fine. I feel resolved.

I'm ready for it. I'm dying.

ANN: What do you mean?

LEDA: I've known for a while but I wasn't ready to tell you.

ANN: What do you mean?

LEDA: Six months ago they weren't seeing much past eight. I've been doing treatments but they haven't been helping. I've stopped the treatments.

ANN: No.

LEDA: This is just how it is.

ANN: If they have a way to make you better you have to take it. It's not up to you.

LEDA: It wasn't making me better.

ANN: And you're telling me now?

LEDA: Annie—

ANN: It's like you don't have any feelings.

LEDA: I have feelings.

ANN: I mean for others.

Silence.

LEDA: I should have told you before. I'm sorry.

ANN: How do I even know you're not just making it up? This is what people like you do. I got married and I'm going to have a baby and you're afraid all the attention is going to be on me.

LEDA: Oh my God, was I like that?

I'm so sorry for what you had to put up with from me.

ANN: This is happening because you turned your back on God.

LEDA: No, this is happening because people die.

ANN: When you turned your back on God you—

LEDA: You promised.

ANN: No I didn't promise.

LEDA: Let's just talk about what's happening right now.

ANN: When you turned your back on God you turned your back on happiness.

LEDA: Maybe some of us don't want to be happy.

ANN: Who wouldn't want to be happy?

LEDA: Those it makes uncomfortable.

ANN: What does that even mean? It sounds so smart but it doesn't mean anything.

LEDA: I just don't know that happiness is the point.

ANN: Come here, come here to me now, come here and put your hands here.

ANN gestures to her belly.

Give me your hands. Put them here.

ANN goes to LEDA.

LEDA: I—

ANN: Put your hands there and know God is here.

LEDA doesn't move.

ANN kneels. LEDA moves away from ANN.

It's time for you to take Christ into your life. He is alive and with us. Pray with me.

LEDA: Annie . . .

ANN: Christ is here with us.

LEDA: Can you tell him I want to be alone with my daughter right now? Do you think he'll grant me that?

ANN retreats. She sits, not looking at LEDA.

I cannot believe what you want me to believe. It's not who I am. It's not who I want to be. It's something I'm not going to do.

ANN: Why not?

LEDA: Because then I'm not afraid. When I admit to myself that I believe in nothing I'm not afraid. That there is nothing but this. That there is no redemption or new life or next life or True life. That there is nothing but this, here, now. Maybe there's goodness and maybe there's some kind of peace, but if there is it has to be here and it has to be now. Me here, you there. That's all. And if you believe something else, then fine. It has nothing to do with me anyway, right? I just need you to let me have my nothing.

Silence.

ANN: What are you asking?

LEDA: I'm asking you to love me.

ANN: I want to see Bud.

LEDA: And I need you to promise you'll love me but you'll leave my soul alone.

ANN: I want to see Bud.

LEDA: *(clearly, calmly, not crying)* I'm glad you have someone who loves you; you deserve that. And I'm glad you're going to have someone to love. When you were born I thought you were going to save my life. I'm so sorry you weren't enough. You can't know how sorry I am. You can't know how much I feel I've lost.

Silence.

Okay. You go see Bud. I'll come in a minute okay.

ANN moves to leave.

Does my hair look okay like this?

ANN: *(lying)* Yeah.

LEDA: I'll come in a minute.

Silence.

ANN: I didn't wear a wedding dress.

LEDA: What did you wear?

ANN: Just a dress. It was green.

It had a little jacket thing. There are pictures.

LEDA: I'd like to see them.

ANN leaves.

LEDA sits on the bed. We can see the deep fatigue she has been hiding.

She closes her eyes.

(like a prayer, a mantra) Open the door. Open the door. Open the door. Open the door. Let the future just be something imagined. That's all it ever was. Calendars and datebooks, appointments made long ago. In three

weeks with the doctor, April with the dentist, a week marked off in red in December that says "vacation." Life doesn't happen in three weeks, in April, in December. Not anymore. Open the door. Open the door. Just here, just now, just exactly now. Fear is nothing but fear. Let the future dissolve with the fear. Now, now, open the door. There will be light, the light is made of love. Open the door, open the door.

LEDA holds her hands up gently before her, her eyes still closed.

Open the door open the door open the door . . .

LEDA opens her eyes. Her hands fall gently into her lap.

Light fades. Music.

In a dim light LEDA departs.

ACT THREE

Music continues.

In a dim light ANN *and* CAROLYN *enter. Light shifts and music stops abruptly.* ANN *is standing in* CAROLYN's *office.*

CAROLYN *stands facing her.* ANN *is no longer pregnant. She wears jeans and a light jacket.* CAROLYN *is dressed casually. A carpet is rolled up, the chairs have been moved and there are cardboard packing boxes on the floor. They are mid-conversation.*

ANN: You're busy.

CAROLYN: I'm just—

ANN: You want me to—?

CAROLYN: No no, I have a minute.

ANN: A minute?

CAROLYN: Yes, no, I have a few moments.

ANN: You're busy.

CAROLYN: A little.

ANN: I called but there—

CAROLYN: Yes, no, the phone's been disconnected.

ANN: You want me to come back later.

CAROLYN: I won't be here later. So, this is good. Your timing is fortuitous.

ANN: "Fortuitous"?

CAROLYN: Lucky.

(moving a box) Let me clear—

ANN: Don't worry about it.

CAROLYN: Everything's all over the place.

ANN: You're moving?

CAROLYN: Yes. Today.

ANN: You're getting another office or whatever?

CAROLYN: I'm going away for a while. I have a little place up north. Small town. In the woods almost.

ANN: You're quitting your job?

CAROLYN: Something like that.

ANN: Do you have a boss?

CAROLYN: No.

ANN: That desk out there, is that where you sit when they first come in?

CAROLYN: No, that's where Margo sat. My assistant.

ANN: Did you fire her?

CAROLYN: She's gone to work for another receptionist—I mean therapist.

ANN: You said "receptionist."

CAROLYN: I meant—

ANN: You meant she was your receptionist.

CAROLYN: Yes. Or "assistant."

ANN: So you're the boss?

CAROLYN: I guess, yes. Was.

ANN: Must be nice. I wouldn't quit a job if I was the boss.

   Silence.

Am I what you expected?

CAROLYN: I didn't expect to meet you.

ANN: But you must have expected something.

CAROLYN: In what way?

ANN: What I'd be like. Or did she not talk about me?

CAROLYN: I'm not supposed to discuss what my clients talk about.

ANN: I thought you quit? And she's dead so she won't care.

Pause.

CAROLYN: Oh.

ANN: You didn't know that?

CAROLYN: No. I haven't seen her since . . . last winter so . . . I'm sorry.

ANN: Why?

CAROLYN: Because . . . I . . . because . . .

ANN: Because that's something that people say.

CAROLYN: I'm sorry I didn't have a chance to speak to her again.

ANN: Yeah well.

Silence.

CAROLYN: Yes she talked about you.

ANN: So am I what you expected?

CAROLYN: I'm not sure.

ANN: I thought you'd be fast.

CAROLYN: Fast?

ANN: Isn't that your job? Figuring people out?

CAROLYN: Partly I guess.

ANN: But you're not very good at it?

CAROLYN: I suppose I expected you'd be like your mother.

ANN: Am I?

CAROLYN: Yes.

Silence.

It was a long way to come, from home.

ANN: I live in the city now.

CAROLYN: Oh.

ANN regards the chairs.

ANN: Where did she sit?

CAROLYN: People sit where they like.

ANN: On TV everybody always has their own chair.

CAROLYN: People can sit where they like.

ANN: Did she mostly sit in one chair?

CAROLYN: *(indicating the first chair)* Mostly there.

ANN sits in the second chair.

ANN: They look comfortable but they're not. Is that so people don't fall asleep?

CAROLYN: Sometimes people have fallen asleep.

ANN: Really?

CAROLYN: Yes.

ANN: Does that make you feel boring?

CAROLYN laughs.

CAROLYN: Maybe.

ANN: Is that your chair?

CAROLYN: Often.

ANN: You don't always sit there?

CAROLYN: No.

ANN: Did you always sit there with her?

CAROLYN: Yes.

ANN: Did you ever go out to dinner or anything?

CAROLYN: No.

ANN: Or talk on the phone?

CAROLYN: Our sessions took place here. Some sessions can happen on the phone, if a client is travelling, or ill. But with Leda our work happened here.

ANN: Leda.

Did she tell you about that?

CAROLYN: About what?

ANN rises, crosses to CAROLYN's chair, sits. Silence.

ANN: Feels the same.

CAROLYN: When did it happen? When did she die?

ANN: Two months. Something like that.

CAROLYN: I hadn't seen her since last February. She missed a couple of sessions and didn't call so I assumed she'd felt her work with me was done, or started seeing someone else.

ANN: "Seeing someone else"?

CAROLYN: Another therapist.

ANN: She came to live with me and Bud.

CAROLYN: You and Bud?

ANN: My husband.

CAROLYN: Oh. I didn't know you were married.

ANN: I'm not anymore. I live here now.

CAROLYN: You and Bud split up.

ANN: Me and Bud. You just heard about him two seconds ago but the way you said "Bud" it sounded like you know him. Do they teach you how to do that?

CAROLYN: Breakups are difficult.

ANN: I left so I'm okay with that.

CAROLYN: And losing your mother.

Silence.

ANN: Did she tell you I was in jail?

CAROLYN: Yes.

ANN: She told everybody. It was no big deal. It was just like a community centre that you weren't allowed to leave. A bunch of women. We played a lot of cards. The food sucked.

CAROLYN: You have strong principles.

ANN: I guess.

CAROLYN: You have a strong faith.

ANN: Is this what therapy's like? Because this is boring.

CAROLYN: A lot of people feel that way. In fact I often feel that way. Which is one of the reasons I don't do it anymore.

ANN: Could I get a glass of water?

CAROLYN: I don't have . . . Everything's packed.

ANN: Don't worry about it.

CAROLYN goes to a cardboard box.

CAROLYN: No I'll just—

ANN: I said don't worry about it.

CAROLYN: It's not a—

ANN: Forget it, I'm fine.

Silence.

CAROLYN: Is there something I can—

ANN: Do you know when her birthday was?

CAROLYN: Leda's birthday?

ANN: My mother's birthday, yeah.

CAROLYN: No.

ANN: So you never went to like dinner or anything.

CAROLYN: No.

ANN: Or to a movie or anything.

CAROLYN: No.

ANN: That would be against the rules?

CAROLYN: In a way yes.

ANN: Did you want to?

CAROLYN: That wasn't part of our work.

ANN: If you went to a movie what movie do you think you might have went to?

CAROLYN: I don't know.

ANN: Right.

Silence.

CAROLYN: Maybe a foreign film. She talked about wanting to go to more foreign films and wishing she had an excuse to go.

ANN: You would have been her excuse?

CAROLYN: Maybe.

ANN: Because you're intelligent?

CAROLYN: Leda was intelligent.

Silence.

ANN: She liked horror movies. She liked getting scared. I used to scare her when I was a kid and she loved that. She was easy to scare. She was scared of lots of stuff. Did you know she was scared of cats?

CAROLYN: No.

ANN: And bicycles. And water. Not like a glass of water but you know. Swimming, the ocean. Did you know that?

CAROLYN: No.

ANN: And Ferris wheels. She was scared of Ferris wheels because one time when she was little her cousin started rocking the seat when they were stopped at the top of one, and she started screaming and he thought she was laughing and so he kept rocking it and rocking it. Did she ever tell you that story?

CAROLYN: No.

ANN: So did you even know her at all?

CAROLYN: We talked more about feelings than facts.

ANN: Being scared of something is a feeling. Isn't it?

CAROLYN: Yes I guess it is.

ANN: But she wasn't scared of dying.

CAROLYN's cellphone rings. She looks at it.

CAROLYN: I'm sorry, I'm going to have to take this.

ANN: I don't care.

CAROLYN: *(on phone)* Hi . . . Yes . . . I'm going to need a little more time . . . I don't know. I'll call you . . . Fine yes good . . . No . . . No that won't be necessary . . . We've discussed this . . . No.

. . . No . . . No. The weather's fine. I know the road, it won't be dark. We've discussed this it's settled. I can't . . . No . . . Yes. Thanks.

CAROLYN hangs up.

Sorry about that.

ANN: Was that a patient?

CAROLYN: They're called clients.

ANN: What's the difference?

CAROLYN: "Client" is more . . .

It's like the difference between an assistant and a receptionist.

ANN: So was that a client?

CAROLYN: I don't have clients anymore.

ANN: So it wasn't one.

CAROLYN: It was a friend. They're helping me with the boxes.

ANN: "They"?

CAROLYN: She.

ANN: A woman.

CAROLYN: Yes.

ANN: What's her name?

CAROLYN: Jane.

ANN: You sounded mad at her.

CAROLYN: I did?

ANN: If somebody talked to me on the phone like that I'd think they were mad at me. Is Jane your girlfriend?

CAROLYN: Why are you asking me that?

ANN: You're a lesbian. My mother told me that. So is Jane your girlfriend?

CAROLYN: Why is that important?

ANN: You don't have to answer.

CAROLYN: It's up in the air at the moment.

ANN: Were you always a lesbian?

CAROLYN: I'm . . . Yes I guess. I was married to a man for some years. Then I met Jane. Do you disapprove?

ANN: I don't care.

CAROLYN: I don't imagine you meet many lesbians.

ANN: I've been in jail, right?

CAROLYN: But I can't imagine your faith approves of—

ANN: Do you have any kids?

CAROLYN: No.

ANN: I do. Lily.

CAROLYN: Where's Lily?

ANN: There, you did it again. "Lily." Like you know her.

CAROLYN: It's a pretty name.

ANN: It's Bud's mother's name. He picked it.

CAROLYN: How old is she?

ANN: Three months.

CAROLYN: So Leda met her.

ANN: My mother was pretty out of it at that point.

CAROLYN: But Lily met Leda.

ANN: She's just a baby.

CAROLYN: She's not with you?

ANN: Do you see her?

Silence.

She lives with Bud's mother.

CAROLYN turns away.

CAROLYN: I should probably—

ANN: So Jane loves you but you don't love her?

CAROLYN: I don't know that that's the case.

ANN: You don't know? How are you supposed to be a therapist for someone else if you don't know something like that about yourself?

CAROLYN: It doesn't work that way. Therapists are often in therapy too.

ANN: That seems stupid. Why would I go to a mechanic who went to another mechanic to fix his car?

CAROLYN: Humans are more complicated than cars, Annie.

ANN: Even that. You say that name "Annie" like you know who that person is. But you don't.

CAROLYN: If you're looking for a therapist—

ANN: I'm not.

CAROLYN: Because I'm not doing that anymore.

ANN: Why not?

CAROLYN: I don't see how that's any of your business.

ANN: What did you do to my mother?

CAROLYN: What did I do to her?

ANN: Do you believe in God?

> CAROLYN *laughs.*

CAROLYN: I see.

ANN: You see what?

CAROLYN: No I don't believe in "God." Certainly not in the sense that you believe.

ANN: What do you know about what I believe?

CAROLYN: It was part of your mother's conversation.

ANN: Did she believe in God?

CAROLYN: I'm sure you know what your mother's beliefs were.

ANN: What were they?

CAROLYN: Probably closer to mine than yours.

ANN: So you don't believe in anything?

CAROLYN: What do you want?

ANN: Nothing.

> ANN *moves to exit, then stops.*

Were you in love?

CAROLYN: Was I in love with Leda?

ANN: Were you in love with my mother?

CAROLYN: No.

ANN: She talked about you like she was in love with you.

CAROLYN: These are particular kinds of relationships, between the therapist and the client.

ANN: Why did she come here?

CAROLYN: I don't know. To understand something.

ANN: About what?

CAROLYN: About you for one thing.

ANN: Tell me something about me.

CAROLYN: About you?

ANN: Yeah.

CAROLYN: You seem angry about something.

ANN: I'm not.

CAROLYN: I don't do this anymore.

ANN: It's like a trick, isn't it?

CAROLYN: A trick?

ANN: It's not really real. I mean, did she know about you and Jane?

CAROLYN: That wasn't part of our conversation.

ANN: Did she know you were married one time? Did she know what kind of movies you liked? Did she know your birthday?

CAROLYN: That wasn't—

ANN: And you didn't know those things about her. So how could you know her.

CAROLYN: I'm not saying I knew her. Leda was a client.

ANN: You didn't even know her name. Her name was Linda. Did she tell you that?

CAROLYN: No.

ANN: She changed her name to Leda when she stopped drinking. Like that was going to make a difference.

CAROLYN: I'm sure it made a difference for her.

ANN: You didn't know anything about her—you didn't know what she liked, you didn't even know her name.

CAROLYN: A person is more than the movies they like; a person is more than their name.

ANN: What is a person?

CAROLYN: I don't know.

ANN: You don't know? Then you suck at your job.

CAROLYN: Yes I did.

Silence.

All people wanted was advice. Or permission. People like your mother wanted to be told what to do and would end up getting frustrated and stop coming or drift away. Other people wanted permission so they'd tell the right stories and make the right breakthroughs in order to give themselves permission to do what they had planned to do all along. It wasn't my job to give advice or permission. My job was to listen and to help people hear what they said. And if I started telling people what to do then I would be failing at my job. But if I didn't give people what they wanted then they'd feel I was failing them. Those were my days. And at night I'd go home and turn on the television and it would seem like every news story was about missing children and border wars and hysterical weather. Then I'd finish off a bottle of wine and congratulate myself for not opening a second. I might sit up in bed and turn the pages of a difficult book in order to feel I was getting through it. I might leave the light on. I might stare at the clock. And with all my will I would try not to let the person beside me in the bed know how utterly alone I felt. These were the nights I understood why people like you pray. Of course people needed advice, of course people wanted permission. How dare I deny them permission? And who was I to tell them what to do?

ANN: You told my mother what to do.

CAROLYN: Yes I did.

ANN: Did you know it was for me?

CAROLYN: For you?

Silence.

ANN: When Bud's dad died I was there. We were all there. Bud and his mom and his brother and me. And he was so scared. All of a sudden he got so scared and he was yelling and sitting up in bed. Bud and Junior had to hold him down. He kept yelling things about being sorry and asking Jesus not to be mad at him. So we prayed and prayed but he kept on going. Then it was like he just got tired. He was too tired to fight anymore and he died. But he was still scared. It was still in his face. Even dead. But when she died . . . When my mother died . . . The last month of it she was out of it most of the time but the last days she kind of woke up. And I wanted to kneel down at her bed to pray so that she would take in God, take in Jesus. But she made me promise that I'd leave her soul alone. She said that before but I just thought, when she's really dying she'll change her mind. But she didn't. So I did what I promised. I just sat by her bed and watched her. She was so peaceful and all the pain was out of her face. Mostly she wouldn't talk but when she would she'd talk about the door is open, now the door is open, smiling and saying the door was open. And one morning she was laying there all peaceful like and beautiful, not beautiful like people say beautiful but beautiful from the inside. Light. And she said, "The door is open." And so I said, "Go through it," because that's the kind of thing you're supposed to say. And she looked at me. Like she could see everything, all of me. Looked right at me and said, "It's for you."

ANN weeps.

CAROLYN goes to a cardboard box. She takes out a box of tissues.

I said it wasn't about her. But it was. Everything I did was about her.

CAROLYN: Leda knew that.

ANN: Her name was Linda.

CAROLYN: Your mother knew that.

ANN: Everything. Everything I did was about her. But who was she?

CAROLYN: I don't think that's the question.

CAROLYN holds out the box of tissues to ANN. ANN takes one.

Silence.

ANN: Do a lot of people cry?

CAROLYN: Yes.

ANN: Did my mother cry?

CAROLYN: Yes.

ANN: Can you help me?

CAROLYN: I don't know.

ANN: Can you try?

CAROLYN reaches out her hand. ANN takes CAROLYN's hand.

Music.

Light fades to black. End.

WAS SPRING

Was Spring premiered at Tarragon Theatre's Extra Space, Toronto, on April 6, 2012, and ran until May 6, with the following cast and creative team:

Kit: Jessica Moss
Kath: Caroline Gillis
Kitty: Clare Coulter

Director: Daniel MacIvor
Dramaturge: Iris Turcott
Set and lighting design: Kimberly Purtell
Costume design: Shawn Kerwin

The play was developed through workshop presentations by Mulgrave Road Theatre, produced by Emmy Alcorn; directed by Ann-Marie Kerr; and performed by Barbara Gordon, Sherry Smith and Jill Anderson.

CHARACTERS

Kit: a girl
Kath: a middle-aged woman
Kitty: an older woman

SETTING

A theatrical reality.
An intimate space.

In the darkness KITTY *enters slowly.*

KITTY: *(in the darkness)* Let there be light.

Light up on KITTY. *She scrutinizes the audience.*

I don't suppose I could get a cigarette?

KITTY regards the audience.

Gawking. Gawking and grinning. Aren't I cute.

KITTY regards a particular audience member.

Remember when you could smoke in hospitals? They had ashtrays by the beds. The nurses would offer you one to calm your nerves. Not anymore.

Ah forget it. Just asking for one's probably enough to get me a fine. Or in handcuffs. Or locked up.

That's what got me here in the first place, asking that nosey little busybody smiley-faced girl from upstairs for a cigarette.

She listens a moment.

Shh.

She listens again.

They'll be back any minute to see if I took my pill. I can take a goddamn pill on my own. "Did you take your pill?" Yeah I took my pill. I took it from under my tongue and put it in my pocket.

She takes the pill from her pocket and inspects it. She puts it back.

Well if I can't get a cigarette can I at least get a cookie? Agh. I don't want a goddamn cookie.

Coconut. Peanut butter. Can't even get a peanut anymore the whole damn world's allergic.

Or a book at least. Could I at least get a halfway decent book?

That nosey little busybody smiley-faced girl from upstairs comes to visit and asks me what she can bring me. I should have known better than to ask her for anything. If I hadn't asked her to get me cigarettes I'd still be at home. But stupid me I ask her to bring me a book and she brings me some paperback book from the hospital store with a cat on the cover.

A cat? Old ladies love cats? Is that as far as she can see?

If I had my way I'd at least have the radio on. I like the radio at night. But apparently it keeps Mrs. Whatshername next door awake. Mrs. what? Mrs. Schnitzler? Mrs. Schnitzler. Mrs. Shitsherself.

KITTY laughs.

"Oh be nice." You be nice. You be nice.

She sings to herself a few lines from an old romantic ballad.

She stops suddenly.

No you won't. No it won't. Not at all. Never not at all.

I asked for a hot chocolate but I didn't get it. Or did I? If I did it wasn't very goddamn good.

She listens a moment.

(quietly) Smiley-face will probably be back with some other book now because she could tell I was less than impressed with the cat-cover book. I doubt she's even read a book in her life. A real book.

Magazines for her I'd say.

Bridal magazines. *Baby* magazines. *Ladies* magazines. I've read real books. Big books. What people would call difficult books. I've read them. Not to say I liked them all but I read them.

Valerie? Or Veronica. Valerie? Yeah well Valerie or Veronica or whatever it is, I've read books. You ever read a book? I doubt it. Valerie? Or Veronica. Vanessa? And so goddamn friendly. Like she knows me. You don't know me.

You don't know me at all. I hung on my doorknob for an hour and a half waiting for someone to walk in. It had to be her though, didn't it. "Can I get you to get me a package of cigarettes?" She's looking past me, inside. "Can I come in?" What was I thinking? That goddamn bucket of pee. You wouldn't think it so strange if you had my knees trying to get up to the toilet. It's just a bit of pee.

Goddamn young people. I can't stand them. I even stopped taking the bus. Full of young people. Where the hell did all the old people go? Poor old fellow upstairs, what happened to him? Then smiley-faced moved in.

Only lived there a couple of months. Never trust a smiley-face. I lived there twenty years. Oh she's so friendly. You don't know me. All I wanted was a package of cigarettes.

"Can I come in?" What was I thinking?

I should have known better but I let her in. Why? And then she sees it, she sees it all. I don't think I even saw it until she came in.

You get used to things. A person gets used to the things they see every day. The way you live. It's just a bit of clutter here and there, a broken window. But then some stranger comes in and it looks like somebody dropped a bomb.

I liked the broken window, I was thinking the garden might grow in through it. Up the walls and over my bed. Eden. Eden overhead.

What really did it was the bucket, that's what did it. It wasn't like I was doing number two in it. It was just pee.

The broken window and a bucket of pee and all I wanted was a package of goddamn cigarettes. Thanks for your help, Veronica smiley-faced-only-lived-here-a-couple-of-months-never-read-a-real-book-in-your-life.

Vanessa? Or Veronica. And I never even got the goddamn cigarettes. Or my hot chocolate. Or a decent book.

Ah fuck 'em all.

> *She looks up a moment.*

No Eden overhead here. And what's going to happen to my rhododendron now? That's something I'll tell smiley-face to do. Water my damn rhododendron.

They told me they wouldn't grow this far north. But I knew that was bull-shit because I remember my mother had them. "Oh but that was in the country," they said. What difference does that make? Dirt's dirt. There's still dirt.

There's still birds. Even here there's birds. Only the morning though. Or I don't know. Maybe there's birds in my brain. But it's not my brain. My brain is fine. Or fine as I can feel it. It's the pain. I wish there were birds in my pain. Go on fly it away, birds. Bye bye, pain.

I expected my lungs but they tell me it's my heart.

She gets lost in a thought for a moment.

We'd go into town on Saturdays. Mother and me. Sugar and flour. One time or two a dress. Fall. One time a movie. A fight with Dad that morning and spent the whole afternoon at a movie in town.

That one . . . Oh come on. You know it. The uncle had the bird. On his arm. The big black bird. The main fellow's uncle. The main fellow, Johnny or Jimmy or Jack something. I loved him. Oh you know it. With the big thing at the end and the . . . What the hell was it? I always loved him. What was his name? You know the movie. Oh I know the name of it.

It'll come if I forget about it.

A moment.

Every Saturday it was town. Mostly to get away from Dad I guess. I had a mean old dad. That was something else I had with . . .

She lets that thought drift away. She looks at the back of her hands.

There'd always be the old man on the corner by the bus. Where the bus came in. "Spare some change? Spare some change?" And now that I think of it he probably wasn't that old. Younger than me now, I'm sure. How old everybody seemed then.

What I see now as bright and smooth and clear-eyed forty then could well have been eighty, eighty could have been Methuselah. I don't look at my face anymore. Sometimes by surprise in a window reflection, in a metal kettle. In the mirror of the lake . . . But that was her. That was then.

I can't find myself. Who is that old woman looking back at me, confused and angry. Though she's not always angry as she looks. She just looks that most of the time now, and that's why she's confused. Who is that? Who is she? And I don't need another angry face to look at, so I don't. I don't need to look at my face to see it because it's all here, my hands, the back of my hands, it's the whole story here. Once they were powder white. Cotton soft. Now, who belongs to these odd things, twenty shades of brown and grey, hanging away from the bone like a too-lose glove. And now it's nothing but more, more and more, nothing but change, lots of change to spare. Nothing but faster down, closer and closer to the earth.

> KITTY *hums a few bars of a song from her youth. She stops. She drifts in and out of a thought.*

"Say your prayers." And to who? That's the joke of it. That's the big joke. Just close your eyes and move your lips. But who the hell are we talking to? I don't know that I believe in anything.

> KATH *appears.*

KATH: Never did.

KITTY: Where's my book?

KATH: How should I know?

KITTY: What?

KATH: What?

KITTY: Oh it's you.

KATH: Yes it's me.

KITTY: I thought you were . . . the smiley-faced one.

KATH: Valerie.

KITTY: I know.

KATH: You look terrible.

KITTY: You're sour as ever.

KATH: You're one to talk.

KITTY: I'm allowed to be sour. I got old.

KATH: We all do.

KITTY: Oh shut up.

KATH: Where's the princess?

KITTY: I thought she'd be with you.

KATH: Why would she come with me?

KITTY: We can't start without her.

KATH: Sounds to me like you already started.

KITTY: I wasn't saying anything. Not for you to hear anyway. Nothing you don't already know.

KATH: Right, "mean old dads" and rhododendrons, that's nothing new. But not believing in anything? Are you finally ready to admit that?

KITTY: I've got nothing to say to you about it.

KATH: Better me than the Princess.

KITTY: What did you tell her?

KATH: I don't talk to her, woman. And it's not up to me to tell her.

(surveying audience; to KITTY) You must have been yakking at them forever. That one looks ready to doze off already.

A candy appears in KATH's hand. She begins to open it from its very crinkly wrapper.

KITTY: What the hell are you doing?

KATH: I'm having a candy.

KITTY: What about everyone else?

KATH: I've only got three.

KITTY: Put that away.

KATH reluctantly puts the candy away.

Selfish as ever.

KATH: Selfish as you.

KIT appears, excited, out of breath.

KIT: Sorry sorry, everybody, sorry I'm late. I had a ride arranged but of course boys will be boys and of course something came up. It's not how I wanted to start—I had an entrance prepared, and a song. I've been taking voice lessons and the teacher says I sing like a bird.

KATH: Yeah, a crow maybe.

KIT: *(to audience)* My teacher herself once sang at Carnegie Hall in New York City.

KATH: At the bar.

KIT: *(to KITTY)* I'm so sorry I'm late—he promised to give me a ride. He has his own car now you know. Have you started already?

KITTY: What do you think?

KIT: Oh, sorry. He promised to give me a ride.

KITTY: The whole world revolves around you. You come in here like a parade. Settle down.

KIT: Sorry. I'm just excited.

KATH: She's always been like that.

KITTY: *(to KATH)* And then you appeared.

KIT: What have you been talking about?

KATH: Why are you talking at all?

KITTY: *(to KATH)* You be quiet.

(to KIT) And you settle down.

KIT: Of course.

(to KITTY) You look nice.

KATH: No she doesn't.

KITTY: No I don't.

KIT: *(to KITTY)* I wore this dress because I know how much you liked it. Remember? And for David.

KATH: Oh great. Let's have a fashion show and talk about him.

KIT: *(to KATH)* Why are you talking to me?

KATH: Why are you talking at all?

KIT: *(to KITTY)* Wouldn't you like to hear my song?

(to audience) I'm just brand new at it but like I said my teacher says I'm very good.

KATH: People will say anything when you're paying them.

KIT: What's that terrible sound?

KATH: What sound?

KIT: Oh it's you.

KATH: I just don't want you to embarrass us.

KIT: God, you don't have an ounce of encouragement in you, do you? I might be good.

KATH: You're not.

KIT: No wonder you were such a horrible mother.

KITTY: *(to KIT)* That's enough of you. And there'll be no singing. What do you think this is, *Reach for the Stars*?

KIT: Fine then.

KATH: That's a relief.

(to audience) You have no idea how grateful you should be.

KIT: It might be better as a grand finale anyway.

KATH: Who do you think you are?

> *The sound of a breeze.*

KITTY: Shhh!

> *All three grow very still and quiet, listening. A perfect afternoon.*

KIT: *(quietly to KITTY)* It's pretty.

KITTY: It is.

KATH: Yes. It was.

KITTY: *(waving the sound away)* I thought it might have been the smiley-face one.

KIT: Valerie.

KITTY: I know.

KIT: *(re: sound)* It's gone.

KITTY: Probably the one next door. Mrs. Shitsher.

KATH: Mrs. Shitsherself.

KITTY and KATH have a laugh at this.

KIT: There but for the grace of God.

KITTY & KATH: *(to KIT)* Shut up.

Silence a moment. KIT takes in the audience.

KIT: Have we done introductions?

KATH: Whatever.

KITTY: Of a sort.

KIT: Really, you two.

(to audience) Well then allow me. I'm Kit. Kathleen but Kit. Short and sweet. Voracious reader and budding musician. I had been considering a future career in social causes—the poor and the starving make my heart break—but now I feel that music is my true calling. I'm an independent person and I have strong opinions and deeply held beliefs. But at the same time I'm no cynic when it comes to love.

KITTY: She's the Romantic.

KATH: That's an understatement.

KIT: She's the Mother. Also Kathleen.

KATH: *(to audience)* I prefer Kath. I tried for Kathy but it didn't stick. I don't have a Kathy demeanour. Kath works better for me. You can say it with a sneer. "Kath." It's not like I choose this state of mind, it's just how I wake up in the morning. I'm not sure why they think of me as the Mother since I'm apparently a terrible one, but *(indicating KITTY)* this one probably thinks of me as the Mother since she hasn't thought of herself or acted like one in a long long time. She's the Old Woman.

KITTY: The Oooooooold Woman.

KIT: You're not that old.

KATH: Yes she is.

KIT: She is not.

KITTY: Yes I am. You want to cut me open and count my rings?

KIT: Ewww.

KITTY: I'm the Kathleen they call Kitty.

KATH: *(disdainfully)* "Kitty."

KITTY: I know I know. I tried for Kathy too. But you get old and you just can't be a Kathy. But Kitty they like. It's cute. And the older you get the cuter they like it. Kate could work, but that's more of a tall, cool drink of water, a Kathleen Hepburn type.

KATH: Katharine Hepburn.

KITTY: What?

KIT: *(to KATH)* Why do you always have to be right?

KATH: Because she's wrong.

KIT: But why do you always have to go around correcting everybody?

KATH: Because they're wrong.

KIT: You're such a know-it-all.

KITTY: *(to KATH and KIT)* Can I finish?

(to audience) For old ladies people like it cute. For old ladies they like "Bunny" or "Poppy" or "Daisy" or "Kitty." I got used to it. Kitty might work if you're with a fellow named "Bruce."

Bruce takes the edge off the Kitty. Kitty and Bruce.

KATH: Let's not get into him.

KITTY: He was my husband.

KIT: I want to talk about David.

KATH: I'm not here to talk about men.

KIT: There's nothing wrong with men.

KITTY: *(to KIT)* You like the men.

KIT: A very particular man.

KATH: Pathetic.

KIT: How am I so different than you?

KATH: How am I no longer an idiot?

KIT: You liked David.

KATH laughs dismissively.

KATH: What difference did that make?

KITTY: *(to audience)* David is the first love.

KIT: *(to audience)* David is my only love.

KATH: *(dismissively)* "Love."

KITTY: *(to KATH)* You shut up.

(to KIT) You go ahead.

KATH: Oh come on.

KITTY: Shhh!

KIT: This is David. A good boy with strong arms and shy to smile and you first notice him in the classroom not because of anything he does but because he's so close to invisible.

First you don't notice his shy smile because he's so much more shy than smile, and first you don't notice his strong arms because shy as he is he keeps himself slouched and covered with his bigger brother's old shirts. His bigger brother who left school the year before or two ago, to drive the tractor on their farm under the eye of their mean old dad.

KITTY: They had a mean old dad.

KIT: Yes they did. And in those first days of David, when I thought of him then, I thought he'd probably end up on the tractor the next year or in maybe two, and he knew that, which is why he sat off by himself. Because why make friends if you're just going to leave, and why find yourself good at science or economics or social anthropology if you're just going to end up next year or two turning dirt under a big green tractor taking orders from your bigger brother and your mean old dad.

KITTY: He had a mean old dad.

KIT: Yes he did. And sitting off there by himself the other girls pay him little attention because he's not showy. He's not on a team and he doesn't speak up at assemblies or run for class president or even make friends with those people who do.

Sometimes that works, if you're not good at a sport or to get up in front of a crowd, sometimes you can just try to make friends with the people who are or who do and then it's like you are, you do, you can. But David doesn't. He doesn't try. He doesn't even pretend to try. He doesn't even pretend to want to try.

And he's not so good to read. The few times he has in class you think you might hear just a little hesitation like a stammer or fear. Being kind the teacher doesn't call on him much. And David is relieved. And so are the other boys.

The girls, they giggle at him with his fearful stammer, all caught up with themselves imagining it was them made him nervous.

But the boys, they know better, his pain is theirs, even the good readers know how close they are to mockery—they know why David is gladly falling back into shadows, away from the bruising judgment of others. They don't call shy painful for nothing. And that is David.

And that would have been all but for one April night in the church hall by the school where they held the dances after the fire in the gym that winter. Even the basketball team played there now. Maybe they'd never build another gym, the scores now so high what with the ceilings so low in the hall. And on a Friday night after the game there'd be a dance.

Mostly the boys out back with roll-yer-owns and braggery, the girls inside all pink meringue in a line against the wall.

And this one April night—and not up front and centre where you'd be sure
to see, but off a bit to one side—there was a couple dancing. The girl was
that scrappy girl with the laugh and the long pants under her dresses in
winter, but the boy, who was he? The scrappy girl you knew was the scrappy
girl because she did her scrappy girl dancing: arms too high, elbows out, a
sharp shuffle, a tight flat grin. But who was this boy? This boy moved like
ink through a glass of water, all fluid and smooth, and if it was a colour
it would be a deep deep blue. That kind of dancing. Not all elbows and
knees and stiff hips like the other boys. This boy danced the way that made
dancing look like trouble to get in. And a closer look and this was David.

How could this be David? Did you ever notice that before, how his hair
fell down over one eye, how his shoulders stretched out broad and down
down to thick strong arms: the kind that might lift you up from crying, or
carry you from a fire, or hold you, hold you forever. And from that night
on it was only ever David you could see.

Who cared about school, the only subject now was David. The only days
that mattered were the days with David in them.

The only view you cared to see was him. How you wormed your way a
thousand ways to be in his line of vision. Changing seats, blaming a head
cold and a draft from the window.

Missing the bus, claiming a lost mitten so you could walk home just far
enough behind him to not be following him. How jealous you became of
the scrappy girl who seemed to be his only friend. So many minutes, so
many days, so many dances. What could one do to make him see you?
Would he ever really see me? And then came the books.

KITTY: All the books.

KIT: He wasn't much to read, you see, but I was.

KATH: Hiding in a book.

KIT: No not hiding. Preparing for life. But David couldn't prepare because he wasn't much to read. So I became his teacher. I'd read his school books for him and tell him the stories. I would sit with him in the field behind the barn past the school. And I'd tell him every story. And he saw the stories. And then he saw me. And then it was spring.

KATH: He saw quite a bit of you behind the barn as I remember.

KIT: Shut up.

KATH: *(to audience)* In the end the scrappy girl got him. I heard he beat her. Just like his mean old daddy did to his mother.

KIT: That's not true.

KATH: And the dancing was fuelled by the booze.

> *A beat.*

KIT: You remember.

KATH: I always remember the drunk violent ones.

KIT: Why do you poison everything?

KATH: Pull your head out of the flower patch, sunshine.

KIT: *(to KITTY)* You liked David.

KATH: He was just another man.

KIT: He was more than that.

KATH: No man's more than a man.

KIT: Is that so? And what makes you the expert?

KATH: All right, you want to know where I stand on men?

(to audience) All right. Here's where I stand with men. And I'm sure every man here is an exception to what I'm about to say. But as far as I've ever found it's like this: babies are born babies: they sleep, they cry, they empty their bottles and fill their diapers. But as they grow they start to show their difference as girls or boys.

Now I'm not sure what starts it, maybe it's a song they hear on the radio, maybe it's the sound of a voice from across the room, maybe it's just when "x" discovers its difference from "y" but things quickly start to change.

And the girl babies start to grow into little princesses that they've learned about from stories of pumpkin coaches and talking mermaids and flying godmothers.

And the boy babies start growing into nicknames like Junior or Slugger or Buddy or Champ and dreaming of race cars and home runs and fire trucks and zombies.

And the little princesses begin to live in hope that someday there will be a prince in the shape of a man, who will save her from feeling like her daddy didn't love her. But the thing is the boys don't grow into princes like the girls need them to—and they do need them to because what good's a princess without a prince? The problem is that the boys, as they grow, don't want to be princes—they want to be kings.

But of course the boy can't become king because Daddy is king and there can only be one king. Of course the truth is that even Daddy isn't king because Daddy's daddy is really king.

And of course Daddy's daddy isn't king because really Daddy's daddy's daddy is king. And it goes on and on and on like that until it turns out there really isn't any king at all.

So what have we got? A world full of princesses and little boys who never grow up. Little boys who dream of kingdoms that will never be theirs and princesses with closets full of pretty ball dresses they'll never get to wear.

KIT: *(to KATH)* It doesn't have to be like that.

KATH: But it is. *(re: KITTY)* Ask her.

KITTY: Don't ask me. *(re: KATH)* I don't know anything about men anymore, not the way she does.

KIT: *(to KITTY)* You know about love.

KITTY: Oh I don't know.

KIT: Try? Try.

KITTY: I remember the lake.

KIT: Oh the lake the lake! Can we go to the lake now?

KATH: *(mocking KIT)* "Oh the lake the lake!" No we can't go to the damn lake.

KIT: Just for a minute!

KATH: No.

KIT: The lake is perfect.

KITTY: Yes the lake. We'll go to the lake. We'll go to the lake together.

KIT: Yes yes, I've been wanting forever to get back there.

KITTY: Deep and black like sleep with no dreams, and the water a smoother smooth than pearls. Getting in the water was just warm enough to welcome you and just chill enough to remind you how you're alive, to set your body singing in the perfect pitch. A temperature like a choirboy's voice. Perfect peace. All this beautiful peace. Just this was enough.

KATH: It's pitiful what age does.

KITTY: Which is?

KATH: Bakes us crusty dry, hiding a mushy filling.

KIT: I think we were speaking of love?

KATH: Up pipes, Sally Sunshine.

KITTY: Love.

KIT: And on that note, there's another thought I have of David—

KITTY: No no no. Not that. No, not that love. That's romance.

KATH: It's not romance, it's a grunt behind the barn.

KIT: *(to KATH)* You have no decency at all, do you.

KATH: *(to KIT)* Oh you're such an orchid.

KITTY: Love. The Love. Real love is when you can for a moment see outside yourself. Hold everything in your hands.

KIT: And he takes you in his arms . . .

KATH: Oh, you idiot, she's not talking about that; she's talking about a daughter.

KIT: Oh.

KATH: *(mocking)* "Oh."

KITTY: I saw it once. There in my hands, perfect and pure.

KATH: Until it becomes twisted by your expectations.

KIT: Stop that.

KATH: Poisoned by your clinging greed.

KIT: Stop it.

KATH: Scarred with your wounds.

KIT: She doesn't want to hear this.

KATH: Before she realizes that all anybody really cares about is what they can get from her. The baby that exists in the calm centre of the storm of our selfishness. While she's this guileless "gift from above." Before she grows up to turn on us. To hate us with such justification. To abandon us with such malice.

KITTY: *(to audience)* Perhaps this could be the child, perhaps this could be the child become a saviour. That moment where it's not even like a person yet. Not a person but so much more and so much less. It's feeling huge, like an airplane to an ant; and tiny, like a pinprick to a planet. Deafening like when you hear your own heart in your head, and delicate as a single snowflake in an empty universe. The connection of everything.

KIT: That's very beautiful.

KATH: *(mocking)* "That's very beautiful."

KIT: What have I done to you to make you like this?

KATH: You only have to ask yourself.

KIT: No really. Your behaviour is acidic. It's inexcusable. What could I possibly have done to you, to make you think your behaviour is acceptable?

KATH: You abandoned me! You left me bitter and biting. That's what you did. And here I end up stuck in the middle. I'm the one who has to live with it all. It's easy for you, you're an idiot. *(re: KITTY)* And it's easy for her, she's drowning in denial.

KIT: Stop that. Be nice.

(to KITTY) Let's go to the lake, come on, it's not that cold. The moon is bright enough; we can bring a blanket.

KATH: *(to KIT)* You don't even know why you're here.

KIT: *(to KATH)* I'm here because I want to be.

KATH: *(to KITTY)* She doesn't even know why she's here.

KITTY: *(to KATH)* She's here because I asked her. That's enough to know.

KIT: *(to KITTY)* Let's say our prayers now. Okay? "Lord, make me a channel of your peace, where there is hatred let me bring your love, where there is . . . " Come on, pray with me.

KATH: She hasn't said her prayers in a long time.

KIT: That's not true.

KATH: She knows better than to waste her time.

KIT: The search for God is never a waste of time.

KATH: I don't seek God. And if I do it's only to blame him.

KITTY: Shhh!

KATH: I would. I do.

KIT: That's hardly helpful.

KATH: If you only knew. It's like her memories: a dirty pond imagined as a black crystal lake. Or you and your wondrous David. All made up. Like a farmer's daughter in a pretty girl's dress. These dreams and promises and plans will abandon you as surely as you abandoned me. What you say you believe means nothing because it will leave you, just as you left me.

KIT: It wasn't me who left.

KATH: You deserted me.

KITTY: You were hardly there enough to leave.

KATH: *(to KITTY)* And then you appeared.

KITTY: I had to. To save you.

KATH: Save me? For what? It's all just an aimless game, a sick joke, an imagined God's cruel sense of humour. You said it yourself, you don't believe in anything anymore.

KIT: She didn't say that.

KATH: Yes she did.

(to KITTY) Tell her.
Tell her.

KITTY: I didn't say that.

KATH: *(to KITTY)* More lies! But what should I expect, it's always been nothing but deceit and denial. Just tell the story, just tell the truth.

KIT: You're scaring her.

KATH: Who's scared?

KIT: *(to KATH)* Remember this dress? You like this dress. How it feels. Touch it. Touch it.

> KATH *does. She moves away.*

KATH: Enough of all that. Nobody cares.

KIT: That I think depends upon how you see the world.

KATH: How can you see anything at all with your head up your arse?

KIT: Do you have to be so vulgar?

KATH: Vulgar? Vulgar? What's more vulgar than you with that dress over your head and your legs in the air in a manure pile behind the barn.

> *A beat.*

KITTY: I can't believe I was ever so miserable as you.

KATH: You still are.

KIT: *(to KATH)* What happened to you?

KATH: *(to KIT)* You did.

(to KITTY) And you keep me here.

KIT: *(to audience)* There are nice stories. Funny stories. Happy stories.

KATH: There's only one story that needs to be told. And it only has one ending.

KIT: There are many stories.

KATH: And they're all the same. We start in innocence. A lie, pretense in a pretty dress, hearing angels in a weedy voice, clinging to the memory of a boy who could see right through you. Steady middle age? No more solid than vapour, than steam. Rising from the iron pot of fear, tightly covered, just about to blow, boiling sheer panic. Wise old age? More like witless, hot chocolate and marshmallows for every meal, warming itself by the light-bulb fireplace. Innocence becomes jaded middle age, middle age rusts into desperation, desperation corrodes into dementia, porous and hollow, like coal, leaving nothing but smoke in the air and dust in your eyes.

KIT: I don't want to listen to this.

KATH: *(to KIT)* But I had to listen to you. I still do. You and your wishes and your dreams. You and your prayers. And what do you pray for? For things, for stuff, for miracles to make life easier, to make the days pass faster, make the nights bearable. Oh yes you prayed, but only ever for yourself. In the beginning every night you went to bed and you prayed that your father would stop drinking and your parents would stop fighting. But they didn't, did they? No. Every night was his hit and rum whispers at your bedside and a symphony of shattering china from the kitchen, fists and hot tears. Was God not listening, or did he just not care? No, you pushed that away—this was meant to be, these are the lessons I need to learn. And on you kept praying. How deluded you are to imagine that God, if he even *is*, that he would care about your self-seeking prayers. Prayers for something pretty to wear. For compliments from strangers. For your David to reappear and rescue you. For "love." For a love just yours.

(to audience) And the true tragedy is that prayers are answered. Suddenly, one sick morning and another and a third and a swelling in our belly. Oh yes, oh yes, I see, I see, you've blessed me finally. Here is the thing that will love me forever, the thing that is mine for all time, the everything and

always of my world. And I believe now, I really do, for a while I believe, because now it seems like there's something to believe in. And I pray for a girl; I pray for a little girl because I don't know how to treat a Junior or Slugger or Buddy or Champ who will never be king and never know why, but a princess I understand, a princess I once was, and maybe this princess I can spare my mistakes; this one will be better, so much better than me. And yes, and she comes and she is. *(indicating KITTY)* It's like she said, that much is true.

There is a moment, there is a time, there is a timeless time where you hold this thing, this tiny thing, and she is perfect and pure; she is the doorway to a feeling of home, but home with no rooms or walls, no doors, no windows, just open space, a perfect pure sense of home. Eyes so clear and full of a picture of what we've always dreamed of but never seen. There is a moment. But the moment ends.

KITTY: It ends when you begin to want. To want to never not lose this. When you hold this feeling in your hands, in your heart, in the eye of your soul, and you know you want it forever. This is what happens, and when this happens, when Want enters, leaning just over your shoulder, whispering in your ear, "What I want, what I want, what I want." That's when the separation starts. Oh there are the lovely days, the tiny tendernesses, you and her on the big veranda, the view of the lake. But the child, the gift, the hope of hope, who once crawled across these floors, slept in your lap on the big veranda, marvelled at your beauty, begins to move away. And the more she moves away, the more she fights against your want, the harder you hold. And then the lie. The lie you tell when you say "All I want is for you to be happy," but the truth is "All I want is to want is to want is to want is to want, forever and always, for you to be mine, to show me all I am and could be." And she knows it, and you know she knows it. And she hates you for it, so you pray, you pray to a God you're not sure you believe in anymore. You pray nights and mornings and in moments of pain. And you try to reach her by giving in to everything. You let her go to the city; you pay for her apartment; you try not to call until you can't try anymore. And when she doesn't answer for two whole days you drive into the city and up and down the one-way dead-end skid-row streets afraid you won't find her. And afraid that you will. And you do. Her eyes vacant and dry, her arms a map of veiny tracks.

But you don't judge her, you don't make demands, you just hand over the money and don't ask questions. And you pretend it is all so selfless. All for her. What I want.

A moment.

KATH: The Thursday before she . . . She came home . . . her arms, covered with pinprick connect-the-dots. You think of a child's puzzle book, a game played with coloured pencils. And then the Sunday. The phone call. The news delivered with a well-practised sympathy. The news. The words. They tell you it wasn't suicide because she didn't leave a note. They said it was an accident. "Accidental." But you know there is a note and you know where to look. That was spring too.

KIT: You like this dress, don't you? Look at me. Look at me.

KITTY looks at KIT.

You like this dress, and you know why? Because the colour brings out my eyes and offsets my skin when I've got a bit of sun. Though I don't have much now because I haven't been to the lake in forever . . . Remember how it was? Remember how brown she got after five minutes in the sun? Remember her shimmering under the surface, popping up slippery and slick all open-mouthed laughing? How it was just you and her and the lake all one. Like you said, perfect.

KITTY: No.

KIT: Yes it was, remember?

KITTY: It's not fair.

KIT: It was so beautiful.

KITTY: *(indicating KATH)* It's not fair to her.

(to KIT) Or you.

KIT: Don't let her ruin everything. She wants to ruin everything.

KITTY: *(to KIT)* I look at you and I say to myself how perfect and gorgeous and lovely you are. But that doesn't mean anything because you don't believe it. All you see is a girl who feels so much but who can't be enough. You waste your time looking, looking, looking for something to make yourself feel how you think you should. Why? You want to please everybody but you know that you can't. It's sad how you want everyone to love you and worse that you don't think you're worth it. All that wasted time. There is no time to waste.

KIT: You're talking like her. Don't.

KITTY: Like you and that damn singing.

KIT: They said I had a gift.

KITTY: But did you ever sing anywhere but alone in your room?

KIT: I will. I'm taking lessons.

KITTY: You don't care about gifts. What you really care about is being seen as a girl with a gift and a calendar full of lessons. Not what you're doing but only what you're dreaming. And you fool yourself that that's the same thing. Oh but it is not.

KIT: David says that dreams are more real than truth.

KATH: Those few short thrusts and a grunt will make everything better.

KIT: You're ruining everything.

KATH: Your dreams will all come true.

KIT: I can't listen to you. I can't even hear you anymore.

KIT turns away, removing herself from the action but with nowhere to go. As the scene progresses she hums quietly to herself. KATH sits silently, turned away.

KITTY: *(to KATH)* And you. You had dreams too. Don't forget that. You got what you wanted. Didn't you? Remember what you wanted? Your big house with your big veranda and your big lake. Where every morning you'd step out of your house onto your veranda and take in your lake. Well it wasn't your lake—you couldn't own the lake—but you could own the view. That house was so big it blocked out the view for the people across the road. Damn you're so selfish you took your view and theirs, that's one big view. And how did you get all that? You married a man you didn't love. That's quite something to do for something you want. And you got it.

Then every morning when you'd walk out of your big house onto your big veranda and look at your big lake, all you would think about is . . .

KATH: What I didn't have.

KITTY: That's right. Because standing there looking out from all you had, onto all you had, all you could think about was what you didn't have.

KATH: Yes.

KITTY: What you wanted.

KATH: I don't want . . . I don't want to feel like this.

KITTY: I know that.

KATH: I want to go to the lake.

KIT turns quickly back.

KITTY: Not yet. Not till sleep.

KATH: And it's almost that now.

KIT: I want the lake.

KITTY: Not yet.

KIT: When?

KITTY: Soon.

KIT: When?

KITTY: Come here.

KIT: I don't like how you talk to me. Neither you nor her.

KITTY: *(to KATH)* Give her a candy.

KATH: A candy?

KITTY: Give her one.

KIT: Are they caramel?

KATH: No they're peppermint. You have a problem with peppermint?

KIT: No I like peppermint better. Caramel gets stuck in my teeth.

KATH: *(to KITTY)* And I guess you want one too.

KITTY: I wouldn't say no.

A candy appears in each of the women's hands.

They each open their candy at the same time. Each very efficiently. Each folding the wrapper into a small square and then tucking it away. Each then pops a candy in their mouth, savours for a moment, then crunches it to ruins.

It's A Wonderful Life. That's the one with Jimmy Stewart.

KATH: A fine looking man.

KIT: And funny.

A moment.

KITTY: I love a hard candy.

KIT: Mmmm.

KATH: The crunch.

KIT: Mmmm.

KATH: I always like to have a few hard candies in my pocket.

KITTY: It's like a grandmother thing to do. Isn't that what grandmother's do? She carries pockets of peppermints and a purse full of quarters and silver dollars. Remember silver dollars?

KIT: Silver dollars, yes.

KITTY: And a dress of tiny flowers and a big soft lap you could climb up into. And a little magnet on a string.

KATH: Fishing for quarters.

KIT: And silver dollars.

KITTY: Crawled up in grandmother's field-of-flowers lap, a magnet on a string, fishing for quarters and silver dollars.

KATH: Getting richer and richer.

KITTY: And walks in the morning.

KATH: Late afternoon.

KIT: Hand in hand.

KITTY: Down the path past the hay field.

KATH: To the lake.

KIT: And safe safe like we were never safe again.

KITTY: I would have liked to have been a grandmother.

KATH: But that's not the story.

KITTY: *(to KIT)* Go ahead.

KATH: *(to KIT)* Go on.

KITTY: *(to KIT)* Go on.

It's all right. Go ahead now.

KIT: But what?

KATH: The beginning.

KITTY: *(prompting KIT)* I was born into a certain unhappiness . . .

KIT: I was born into a certain unhappiness. Not unlike the usual unhappiness most people live with. Nothing fit for a film or a book, a boring sort of unhappiness. Although sometimes it did seem my parents were a partnership of alcohol and argument I managed to survive.

I was an only child, which may have stoked this fire of loneliness which I seem to have always carried. I was the daughter and a good daughter in hopes that this would make my parents happier. And even though I tried and I said my prayers every night and I made all the right choices and brought home all the best grades, unhappiness persisted.

My unhappiness was mostly hidden, even from myself. Hidden behind a mountain of books—which truth be told was more a hill of romance—and hidden by a dream of music, which, truth be told, was more of a fantasy than an ability.

My teacher called me gifted but she said that to everyone, even that stuck-up rich girl from over the road with the scratchy-fingernails voice.

KATH: And then a boy.

KIT: And then a boy. A boy who danced like elastic and joy. Who wouldn't even see the big girl. And the more he wouldn't see you all you wanted was him. Music didn't matter anymore, books became just paper, days were all the same and bundled as weeks, and you didn't care anymore about wanting to be good.

So you used all your precious hill of romance, your paper mountain became research, and you showed him how easy it would be to take you. And he took you. But he wouldn't keep you. And there was nothing you could do. And there was no one you could tell. You were gone. You looked in the mirror and you were no longer a child.

KATH: I was a woman.

KITTY: A woman with a baby in my belly and no man to name it. And then came Bruce. Bruce, a man physically, yes, but if you were to imagine gallant or steadfast, heroic or stalwart as the making of man, he was none of these. Although he had ambition and was well set to climb a ladder at the bank. So let's call him at least male. He was the other side of David in all ways. But Bruce was lonely enough to be willing, and concerned about appearances enough to be quiet.

He was good with numbers and honest in the bank but he allowed himself the indulgent deception of not counting the difference between six and nine months where conception might matter. Now my setting was in place. But the money from the bank and the position in town and friends from the county and a big lot by the lake where no one had built. And there we were, the man I didn't love, and my veranda and my view. But none of that mattered because all my hopes turned to the one thing I couldn't see:

KITTY, KATH & KIT: The baby in my belly.

KITTY: This was the thing crystalline clearest to me: this would be my one, this would be forever, this my centre, my point, my reason to be.

KIT: She would be . . .

KATH: She would be . . .

KITTY: She would be everything I couldn't be. But where it went wrong was that she wasn't me. And she didn't want to be. My little me who wasn't me and didn't want to be.

A beat.

They didn't call it suicide because she didn't leave a note. But I knew.

KATH: But I knew. And I knew where to look. Straight into the mirror. And then a numbness. But to everyone around you it is sharp and bitter and burning to touch.

And some very quickly and some slowly but soon mostly everyone is gone, bruised and cut and burnt enough. But I am asleep through it all. A restless numb sleep. And when I finally jolt awake it is into a burning delirium of grief.

When I come upon the few brave souls remaining around me I do everything I can to smother them in blame. That is my comfort and my disease, blame. And now my husband is gone and my daughter is dead and blame is my house and my garden, it's my sun-up and dusk, only blame to fill the darkness when I turn out the light. Blame is everywhere making my world so small that now I am smothering myself. And the darkness is everywhere. Tiny and finite but endless. All that's left now is whiskey in the morning, Scotch for lunch and wine with dinner, but dinner is ruined. What to do now? Don't worry, drown your disappointment with vodka and ice. These are the days, the days become numbers, the numbers just ounces in bottles, and these are the every damn day is the same days.

No daylight, no dusk, no midnight, no dawn, no person friend nor foe, no God, neither of mercy or vengeance. I am hopelessness. My child is dead and I feel more a mother than I ever did.

KITTY: Oh salt oh salt oh bring me salt for these wounds, open the sky and pour salt on my flesh, my open heart. My pain is all pain, my wound is an empty ocean, a frozen lake, my loss is the dust of dust of dust.

KATH begins to hum a song from her youth. After a time:

KIT: *(to KITTY)* Don't be afraid.

KITTY: No?

KATH: No.

KITTY: One more trip to the lake?

Gently we hear the sound of the lake. Through the following KATH and KIT speak to KITTY.

Black and warm in spots and so icy cold in others.

KATH: One perfect afternoon. It was spring.

KITTY: The perfect mix of sun and shadow.

KATH: The shimmering stillness.

KITTY: The sound of blue and green.

KIT: And she was there.

KATH: She was there.

KITTY: She was always there.

KIT: I was.

KATH: We were.

KITTY: I was always there.

And together she and I are floating in the lake, long enough that we become water, us and the lake the same thing.

KIT: She was a little fish.

KATH: Her fingertips wrinkled like raisins.

KIT: We lay on the dock.

KITTY: For hours of afternoon.

KATH: In the cool dark slashes of shadow that lined the dock.

KITTY: And listen.

KIT: Just listen.

KATH: Listen.

KITTY: To dreams.

KIT: To nonsense.

KATH: Wonderful nonsense.

KITTY: Listen so hard I am breathless.

KIT: Had anyone ever talked to me this way, this much?

KATH: Needed my listening so.

KIT: A perfect afternoon.

KATH: A perfect afternoon.

KITTY: Perfect.

KATH: How could anything ever be this perfect?

KITTY: A lake cold and warm.

KATH: A tiny waterfall and a brook at one end.

KIT: Running laughing screaming from frogs.

KATH: The other end rocks we called a cliff.

KITTY: Halfway to heaven.

KATH: And we climb the tiny cliff at the far end of the lake and lie on its flat rock table top, and on our backs there we with our fingertips trace and make sense of the clouds.

KIT: A perfect afternoon.

> *KIT and KATH quietly sing the song from their youth as KITTY continues.*

KITTY: Between April and June is the time for rhododendrons. Soon. And they require some sun. A first floor apartment with a door to a garden. It wasn't a garden when I got it. But there was dirt. And a bit of sun. I think I took the place for the sun. And the dirt. For the rhododendron. And Mother grew them. They require effort. Concern. And I could have had the window fixed, the broken window, but it was silly me, I guess, imagining the blossoms up the wall. On the ceiling. Eden overhead.

"Can I come in?"

Come in. Come in.

> *KATH and KIT are gone.*

I do believe in something.

I believe in spring.

> *KITTY sings a bit of the song from her youth.*

Light fades until she is tiny and alone.

KITTY looks into the audience as if for someone she recognizes. She grows nervous. Then resolved. She rises and steps toward us.

It is spring. Black.

End.

Blackout. End.

SMALL THINGS

Small Things had its world premiere as a commission from Prairie Theatre Exchange in Winnipeg from October 16 to November 5, 2015, with the following cast and creative team:

Patricia: Barbara Gordon
Birdy: Ellen Peterson
Dell: Alissa Watson

Director: Robert Metcalfe
Dramaturge: Iris Turcott

The play had a public workshop at the Chester Playhouse in Chester, Nova Scotia, in July 2015, produced by Mary Lou Martin, with the following cast:

Patricia: Deborah Allen
Birdy: Heather Rankin
Dell: Andrea Lee Norwood

CHARACTERS

Patricia: retired, well-bred, was a schoolteacher and administrator in the
city, formal
Birdy: grew up in this town, good-natured but pugnacious
Dell: Birdy's daughter and a mother of two, smart but drifting

DESIGN

While encouraging minimalism it might be helpful to see Birdy's environment gently growing neater as Patricia's grows gently messier.

This might be represented in dress as well.

ACT ONE
SCENE 1

Friday afternoon.

PATRICIA's sitting room. She is in her comfortable chair reading BIRDY's resumé, making notations in a small notebook with a pencil. A cane leans nearby.

BIRDY sits across from PATRICIA in a formal sitting chair, her windbreaker on, her purse in her lap.

Some time passes. PATRICIA plays with her pearls as she studies the resumé.

PATRICIA makes a note. She returns to reading the resumé. She erases her note, making a correction.

Finally:

BIRDY: Sorry I was early. I'm always early.

PATRICIA: It was a little uncomfortable for the lady before you.

BIRDY: Oh Elaine's always uncomfortable.

PATRICIA: You know her?

BIRDY: I know everybody.

PATRICIA makes a note in the notebook.

PATRICIA: "Birdy"?

BIRDY: Bernice, but everybody calls me Birdy.

PATRICIA: As opposed to "Bernie"?

BIRDY: Bernie?

PATRICIA: It would be the obvious diminutive.

BIRDY: Right. Yeah.

If you give me the job you can call me whatever you want.

PATRICIA makes a note in her notebook.

But probably not Bernie though, if you don't mind.

PATRICIA: Very good.

BIRDY: You said on the phone you were living in the city. Why'd you move out here to hicksville?

PATRICIA: I looked at a number of towns about this distance from the city.

BIRDY: The prices are crazy here.

PATRICIA: The prices?

BIRDY: If Sean and me were buying our house today there's no way we could afford it. People are moving out here from the city and paying way more than anything's worth and driving the prices up.

PATRICIA: Do you imagine I'm one of those people?

BIRDY: No no, I'm sure you know what things are worth. No, other people. Young people.

PATRICIA: Well you'll benefit, won't you, should you decide to sell your house to some young people.

BIRDY: Oh God, nobody'd want to buy my house.

PATRICIA: Very good.

PATRICIA goes back to the resumé.

BIRDY: I guess. I mean why'd you leave the city?

PATRICIA: My husband passed away.

BIRDY: Mine too.

PATRICIA: I'm sorry to hear that.

PATRICIA consults her notebook.

Very good.

BIRDY: And away from the bustle.

PATRICIA: Pardon me?

BIRDY: All the business of the city.

PATRICIA: That bothers some people.

BIRDY: And dirty. It's got so dirty. Last time I was in, Patricia? Sean and me went to some park and there was—

PATRICIA: Actually, Mrs. Branch, if you don't mind.

BIRDY: Oh.

PATRICIA: For now. I was a schoolteacher so I'm comfortable with Mrs. Branch.

BIRDY: Gotcha.

Teachers were always like that to me anyway. I imagined their husbands even called them Mrs. Morrison or Mrs. Terrant.

Of course they all had nicknames. Did you?

PATRICIA: Did I?

BIRDY: Have a nickname?

PATRICIA: Not to my knowledge.

BIRDY: I bet ours didn't know either.

PATRICIA: I see by your resumé you haven't been working for some time.

BIRDY: I didn't need to work. Then Sean died.

PATRICIA: Of course.

BIRDY: He had insurance from the plant for a while. Right out of school he got that job. And he loved cars so engines was perfect. They make engines up there right? Different certain parts, not the whole engine. Sean was on quality control.

PATRICIA: Very good.

BIRDY: And then my daughter Dell moved back home with her two boys.

PATRICIA: Can you tell me a little about your experience?

BIRDY: With Dell?

PATRICIA: With housekeeping.

BIRDY: Oh. Well I've been cleaning houses all my life of course, but there's all that other stuff too that you read there. A year at the Grace and a year at St. Margaret's. I did almost half a year of nursing before I met Sean.

PATRICIA: Very good. You're fine if I call your references?

BIRDY: Call my references?

PATRICIA: When one is looking for fuller care it's important that both sides of the job are met with equal attention.

BIRDY: Right.

PATRICIA: It's important that you know how to clean a floor.

BIRDY: I know how to clean a floor.

PATRICIA: So do you mind if I call your references?

BIRDY: Oh . . . Um . . . Can I take a look? Dell put all that together for me.

PATRICIA: Dell?

BIRDY: My daughter. Dell. She lives with me. Her and her boys.

PATRICIA hands BIRDY the resumé. BIRDY takes a look.

That one's good.

I think that one's dead. But there's someone in the office who'll vouch for me.

And that one's my nephew. He's not on there because he's my nephew, I took care of his wife's mother for a few months at the end. I probably wouldn't have put him on there since he's my nephew. But we're not that close that he'd lie.

BIRDY hands back the resumé.

PATRICIA: That's good to know.

So five days a week, duties consist of grocery shopping, laundry, general housework, keeping an eye on my medications, that sort of thing.

BIRDY: And personal care.

PATRICIA: As time may dictate.

BIRDY: Gotcha.

PATRICIA: "Gotcha"?

BIRDY: Gotcha.

PATRICIA: Very good. You have a licence?

BIRDY: For nursing?

PATRICIA: For driving.

BIRDY: Oh yeah.

PATRICIA: There may be some driving in time.

BIRDY: I'll get you where you gotta go. I got a great little bomber.

PATRICIA: I have a car.

BIRDY: What kind?

PATRICIA: An Audi.

BIRDY: Big?

PATRICIA: It's an older model.

BIRDY: I got a Civic. Sean never had to touch it and it ran on a dime. It's rusting out a bit on the bottom. Sean said do the undercoat but I thought it was just a way get more money out of us. Me being cheap again. Always undercoat. Worth every penny.

PATRICIA: Very good. I think we're done.

I'll let you know. I'm conducting a number of interviews.

BIRDY: Who are you interviewing?

PATRICIA: Who am I interviewing?

BIRDY: Besides Elaine.

PATRICIA: I don't think—

BIRDY: I just mean I know all the girls, that's all, that would be applying for this job. Elaine MacDonald, Susan AuCoin, Big Jessica.

PATRICIA consults a list in her notebook. She looks at BIRDY.

PATRICIA: Go on.

BIRDY: Elaine's nice. Did you mind the twitch?

PATRICIA: The twitch?

BIRDY: You know, like this.

BIRDY demonstrates a brief twitch.

It bothers some people. Doesn't bother me. It's not permanent they think.

Did you see Stinky yet?

PATRICIA: Stinky?

BIRDY: Susan AuCoin.

PATRICIA: Yes.

BIRDY: It's okay, she calls herself Stinky. We used to think it was something she ate but the whole family smells that way. You can mention it, she knows.

PATRICIA consults her notes.

PATRICIA: Monica Bona.

BIRDY: Monica Bona. Oh yeah.

PATRICIA: What?

BIRDY: I don't like to gossip.

PATRICIA: But?

BIRDY: I'll just say Monica's fine if you don't leave her alone in a room. Sticky fingers.

PATRICIA consults her list.

PATRICIA: Jessica—

BIRDY: Big Jessica.

PATRICIA: Jessica Fraser.

BIRDY: The one on oxygen.

PATRICIA: Yes.

BIRDY: From the smoking. She still climbs stairs though, slow but she gets there.

After a moment.

PATRICIA: How would you clean a floor?

BIRDY: On my hands and knees.

PATRICIA: As would I.

BIRDY: The only way to clean a floor.

After a moment.

PATRICIA: I'll see you Monday.

SCENE 2

BIRDY's living room. That night.

DELL sits on a sofa. She is rolling a joint over a magazine in her lap. She takes great care; she has done this often.

BIRDY enters. DELL drops the joint in the magazine and casually flips through it.

BIRDY: What are you doing?

DELL: Nothing.

BIRDY: Nothing?

DELL: Nothing.

BIRDY: Are the boys in bed?

DELL: You saw me put the kids to bed an hour ago.

After a moment.

BIRDY: I could have been a teacher.

DELL: Are we still going over this?

BIRDY: I'm just saying I could have been a teacher.

DELL: I know.

BIRDY: I coulda done that.

DELL: I know.

BIRDY: Your aunt Maddy too but she picked secretarial school.

DELL: I know.

BIRDY: I was all set for nursing.

DELL: But Dad wouldn't let you.

BIRDY: He wouldn't not let me. He wouldn't *not let me*.

DELL: He wouldn't let you go later when you wanted to.

BIRDY: No. Not *let me*. Where are you getting that?

DELL: I'm glad you got the job.

After a moment.

BIRDY: I could have been a teacher. But I hated school. Mrs. Morrison. Mrs. Terrant. Those kind of teachers. Ugh.

The way she says very good. When you tell someone something and they say back "Very Good." Not like it really is very good, not like "go on." That's the difference between a good teacher and bad teacher. A good teacher says very good a way that makes you want to tell more and a bad teacher says very good like slamming a door.

DELL: If you don't like her don't take the job.

BIRDY: Why'd you put Jeremy to contact? That looks bad that he's my nephew.

DELL: Why? You worked for him, didn't you?

BIRDY: You don't put family on a list like that. Might've lost me the job.

DELL: But you got the job. Why does "might've" matter? Like saying you might've died. You died or you didn't.

BIRDY: What are you talking about dying for?

DELL: I'm just saying . . . Forget it.

After a moment.

BIRDY: You should take those boys to church.

DELL: To church?

BIRDY: Children should have some kind of instruction.

DELL: Remember what happened when you took me to midnight Mass that Christmas? What was I? Five?

BIRDY: Four or five.

DELL: That big crucifix at the front over the altar. And I look up at the statue of the man on it . . .

BIRDY: That crucifix was too real looking.

DELL: . . . and I said, "Who is that?" and you said, "That's Jesus."

BIRDY: And you howled, "I thought Jesus was a BABY!"

BIRDY laughs.

You had a fit. I had to take you out.

After a moment.

And try and get a laugh out of her? Sour. Sean would say you couldn't get her to crack a smile for a kick in the leg.

DELL: What does that even mean?

BIRDY: It means she wouldn't even smile.

DELL: She wouldn't laugh at your dumb jokes.

BIRDY: You watch yourself.

After a moment.

And trust me she's going to need more than help with housekeeping soon enough. That cane's going to be a walker soon enough. And I had to tell her things five times.

DELL: You say everything five times.

BIRDY: *Do* I?

After a moment.

Somebody's got to work. Can't just sit around here all day.

DELL: I'm starting that course.

BIRDY: It's not much of a course if you don't have to leave the house.

DELL: It's an accredited college.

BIRDY: How can it be a college without a building? A college has classrooms and a cafeteria and trees and parking spots, that's a college. What are you going to do, Dell?

DELL: I'm raising two kids.

BIRDY: I guess.

DELL: You guess? You guess? Wow.

After a moment.

BIRDY: You don't let kids make the law.

DELL: What's the law?

BIRDY: Well if you don't know that's the problem.

DELL: Yes, Dad.

BIRDY: Sense is sense.

After a moment.

DELL: And try not talking her to death.

BIRDY: Talking her to death? Oh my God.

DELL: Leave some space for other people to talk.

BIRDY: Leave some space for other people to talk? Leave some space for other people to talk? I talked to the woman today. We talked. She said plenty. I got the job. I'm the one who got a job.

DELL: I'm trying to find something that fits my schedule.

BIRDY: What was wrong with the sub shop?

DELL: I got that rash.

BIRDY: From the sauce?

DELL: Yes.

BIRDY: Everybody eats it all the time and they're fine, but you get a rash from touching it?

DELL: I don't know how fine everybody is, the hospitals are full.

BIRDY: I doubt that's from the sauce on the subs Dell. If you're looking for a reason for a rash I'd look at that stuff you're smoking day and night.

BIRDY rises to leave.

DELL: Yeah yeah.

BIRDY: And you're not smoking that in the house.

DELL: What?

BIRDY: I can smell it Dell. Unless they're putting pullouts for it in the magazines now.

DELL: No I'm not smoking it in the house.

BIRDY: You shouldn't be smoking it at all.

DELL: It's medicinal.

BIRDY: For what?

DELL: Living with you.

BIRDY: Well what do I get to take for living with you?

BIRDY exits. After the coast is clear DELL takes out the joint.

(calling from off) Not in the house!

SCENE 3

PATRICIA's sitting room. The first morning.

BIRDY stands in her coat, her purse over her shoulder, holding a fern.

PATRICIA sits in her chair, a book open in her lap.

PATRICIA: What's that?

BIRDY: It's a fern.

PATRICIA: I'm not much for plants.

BIRDY: It's just a fern.

PATRICIA: I'm not much for ferns.

BIRDY: Oh.

PATRICIA: Just put it down somewhere, it's fine.

BIRDY: Really?

PATRICIA: Pardon me?

BIRDY: Do you not want it?

PATRICIA: No, it's fine, just put it down.

BIRDY puts the fern down.

BIRDY: Thank you.

PATRICIA: Shall we run through how things work.

BIRDY: How things work?

PATRICIA: How things work.

BIRDY: Do you have one of those computerized washers? One of those crazy coffee machines?

PATRICIA: I prefer tea.

BIRDY: Well I know how tea works.

PATRICIA: When I say how things work I'm not referring to "things" per se.

BIRDY: Things per say?

PATRICIA: No.

BIRDY: Oh.

PATRICIA: I mean how *it* works.

BIRDY: How *it* works?

PATRICIA: Here with us.

BIRDY: Oh.

Should I sit down?

PATRICIA: That won't be necessary.

BIRDY: Do you want your tea first?

PATRICIA: Now? No.

BIRDY: Is there some special time you like your tea?

PATRICIA: Yes in fact. In the morning and at tea-time.

BIRDY: Tea-time.

PATRICIA: Yes.

BIRDY: Which is when?

PATRICIA: Fourish.

BIRDY: Four or fourish?

PATRICIA: Around four.

BIRDY: Before four, around four or after four around four?

PATRICIA: Perhaps a little after four.

BIRDY: How little after?

PATRICIA: At *tea-time*. With cookies or a bit of cake.

BIRDY: Oh tea-time yeah, gotcha. My gramma used to do that. It reminded her of the war she said.

PATRICIA: Very good. There's a smock in the laundry room.

BIRDY: A smock?

PATRICIA: Yes. It may be a little big but we can have it taken in.

BIRDY: A uniform?

PATRICIA: A smock.

BIRDY: I'm good like this.

PATRICIA: It's for your convenience.

BIRDY: I'm good like this.

PATRICIA: You wouldn't have to worry about ruining your clothes.

BIRDY: Oh this is just my cleaning clothes, they can get mucked up.

PATRICIA: But with the smock you wouldn't have to wear cleaning clothes.

BIRDY: What would I wear?

PATRICIA: Whatever you'd wanted since you'd have the smock.

BIRDY: But I don't need the smock because I've got my cleaning clothes.

PATRICIA: We can discuss this later.

BIRDY: We're discussing it now.

PATRICIA: Fine.

Are you uncomfortable driving a larger car?

BIRDY: No no, I'll drive anything. I dove Sean's truck all the time. Dell's got that now.

PATRICIA: Dell?

BIRDY: My daughter?

PATRICIA: Yes yes of course, and grandsons.

BIRDY: Well they don't drive the truck, they're only six and eight. Poe would though I bet. He's eight. In a second if you gave him the chance. Poe! I know, don't ask me. I mean I said to her, "Poe? Imagine what the kids'll do with that in school." But he doesn't have any trouble at school though. He doesn't take anything from no one. Tough. You'd have to be I suppose with a name like Poe.

PATRICIA: And the six-year-old?

BIRDY: Wolfgang. I know, I know, don't talk to me talk to Dell.

PATRICIA: What does Dell do?

BIRDY: Oh she's on about "taking a course." On the computer? Taking a course in solitaire maybe. Taking a course while she's watching a movie. Don't get me started. Do you have any kids?

PATRICIA: Shall we get on with the day?

BIRDY: So is that all how it works?

PATRICIA: We'll see how it works.

BIRDY: Let's do that.

> *BIRDY exits. PATRICIA picks up her book. We hear a vacuum cleaner from off. PATRICIA glares off in the direction of the noise.*

SCENE 4

BIRDY's living room. DELL *lies on the sofa reading a magazine.* BIRDY *enters, returning home.* DELL *sits up and grabs a textbook.*

BIRDY: Don't even ask. Don't even ask me.

DELL: What?

BIRDY: How was my day? Don't even ask me. What are you doing?

DELL: Reading.

BIRDY: Oh God, I can't get away from it.

DELL: What?

BIRDY: That's all she does all day, her head in a book.

DELL: There's nothing wrong with reading.

BIRDY: What are you reading?

DELL: It's for my course.

BIRDY: Oh God, don't start with me tonight, Dell, all right.

DELL: What?

BIRDY: First she's got me in a uniform—I'm not wearing a uniform, I put my foot down there.

DELL: What kind of uniform?

BIRDY: Oh this blue thing. I'm not wearing a uniform. And "tea-time tea-time tea-time." She has *tea-time.* Get real, it's a cup of tea and a square. She's like your great nanny. Likes to put on a show. "We'll see how it works." Yeah well, we'll see how it works for me too. And I can tell you she's not going to let go of me having to call her "Mrs. Branch."

DELL: That's her name.

BIRDY: She's not my teacher. And what do I know about her? Nothing. Any kids? No idea. What did her husband do? God knows if I don't. Not a word of anything. Face in a book all day. The only time she almost perked up was when I talked about the boys.

DELL: Can we talk about Alice?

BIRDY: Stop it.

DELL: He wants to be called Alice.

BIRDY: Stop it, Dell, not tonight.

DELL: We're going to have to talk about it sometime, Mom. He won't answer if you don't call him Alice.

BIRDY: Well if you hadn't called him Wolfgang in the first place he wouldn't have had to go looking for another name.

DELL: It's not about his name, Mom.

BIRDY: They tried to call me Bernie; they called me Bernie until high school. They'd still be calling me Bernie now but that I didn't like it.

DELL: So?

BIRDY: I'm just saying I didn't like Bernie but it was nothing to do with it being a boy's name. I went to school with a girl who had a sister Charlene they called Charlie. I would have liked Charlie. There was a perfume "Charlie." That would've been fine.

DELL: What's your point?

BIRDY: I'm saying if I liked Bernie I'd be Bernie today. It's not about anything but that. I'm saying a name is a name. It's not about anything but what you call somebody. Pick some other name.

DELL: It's not about his name, Mom.

BIRDY: You could start maybe by reading him some stories with boys' names in them.

DELL: This has nothing to do with the stories I read him or the movies he sees.

BIRDY: You're always showing him girl's movies. *The Little Mermaid* is not for boys.

DELL: This is not about me.

BIRDY: Oh come on. Come on. You're his mother. Who is it about? Him? He's a kid. You're the one who makes the rules; you're the one who sets the law down. Everybody today making it about the kids. Ridiculous. That's just lazy.

DELL: Lazy? I'm lazy?

BIRDY: I'm not saying you.

DELL: If I knew what to do I would do it.

BIRDY: Just let it be. It'll go away.

DELL: Let it be?

BIRDY: Yes.

DELL: I think that's what's called lazy.

BIRDY: Well you keep pretending to read your book there, and your lazy mother is going to make herself a bite to eat before she faints after her long hard day of cleaning some stuck-up old-bag rich lady's house.

> *BIRDY exits. DELL tosses the book aside. She takes a joint out of a small container nearby. She looks at it but doesn't light it. She stares off, confused.*

SCENE 5

PATRICIA's sitting room, the next afternoon. PATRICIA is reading. BIRDY enters taking off rubber gloves, her purse under her arm.

BIRDY: So I put in a load of towels and I'm going to wait for the sheets till tomorrow.

PATRICIA: That's fine.

BIRDY: And I did the bathroom. I'm going to pick up some Vim. You need something grittier to clean the bathroom, that eco stuff doesn't get rid of the water stains. We've got hard hard water here and it stains like a bugger on the sinks and the toilets. Vim is beautiful, does a beautiful job. But I did the bathroom up as best I could with that eco stuff.

PATRICIA: That's fine.

BIRDY: Next I'll run the vacuum over the carpets.

PATRICIA: That's fine.

BIRDY sits and takes her lunch from her purse.

BIRDY: I'm going to have my lunch now.

PATRICIA: Pardon me?

BIRDY: Break time. Don't worry I brought my own.

BIRDY arranges vegetables and dip.

Dell's got me on this crazy diet. For my digestion.

After a moment.

Have you heard of giving people pot for glaucoma?

PATRICIA: Have I heard?

BIRDY: The pot for glaucoma? That they give it to people. Doctors do. I mean you can get a doctor to do anything for a price apparently. Sean's cousin had this awful little dog, some kind of terrier type. Awful. Mean. And she got some doctor to make out some certificate to say it was what do they call it . . . Oh you know . . . Like a Seeing Eye dog . . . Or one of those dogs that turn on the lights for people who can't— Not that she needed one, I mean there was nothing wrong with her really. Anxiety she said. "The dog was good for her anxiety." I never saw any of her anxiety. Lots of selfish though. Selfish girl. Maybe anxiety is what they call selfish now. Looks like that if you ask me. Oh come on . . . Like a worker dog . . . What do they call it?

PATRICIA: A service dog.

BIRDY: No.

PATRICIA: Yes.

BIRDY: No not that.

PATRICIA: A service animal. A service dog.

BIRDY: No.

PATRICIA: Fine then.

BIRDY: Or maybe yeah. Maybe. Service dog? Yes right maybe yes. Service dog. But it was just so she could take it everywhere with her. I'm telling you, that dog was of no service to anything but noise. Apparently twelve hundred dollars and it was a done deal. Got a licence for it. Money makes the world go round. And of course Dell's all on about this medical marijuana nonsense. As a business. People can apparently get a licence for a business selling it. What do you make of that?

PATRICIA: Not something I think about.

BIRDY: Me neither, if it wasn't for Dell.

After a moment.

I had a look at your car. It is big.

PATRICIA: It was my husband's. It's an older model.

BIRDY: Dell's got mine today.

PATRICIA: Um hm.

BIRDY: Taking Poe to the doctor. To get his cast off. Broke his arm. Fell out of a tree. He's a climber.

After a moment.

(re: her lunch) Gerbil food.

After a moment.

I'll have my lunch then I'll run the vacuum over the carpets.

PATRICIA: You don't need to tell me what you've done, what you're doing or what you're about to do. I trust that you'll get the job done.

BIRDY: All right.

PATRICIA: All right?

BIRDY: All right.

After a moment.

I'm going to move that fern to get it some more light.

PATRICIA: I'm reading.

BIRDY: I see that.

PATRICIA: I would just prefer a little less prattle.

BIRDY: A little less prattle?

PATRICIA: Yes.

BIRDY: Prattle?

PATRICIA: Yes.

BIRDY: You want me to prattle less?

PATRICIA: If that would be all right?

BIRDY: Okay.

After a moment.

PATRICIA: I'm going to finish my chapter.

BIRDY bites loudly into a carrot.

SCENE 6

BIRDY's living room.

DELL lies on the sofa, blanket over her, reading a magazine. As BIRDY enters DELL continues reading the magazine.

BIRDY: What kind of car is an Audi? German?

DELL: I think.

BIRDY: It's a boat.

DELL: Uh-huh.

BIRDY: She says they're known for their "fine engineering."

DELL: I guess.

BIRDY: La-de-da. That Civic? There's fine engineering. Sean never went near those European cars. He said never touch a car you can't take apart. And listen, I know I can talk okay, I know that, but don't call it prattle. Prattle? What kind of word is that to say to someone?

DELL: Uh-huh.

BIRDY: And hiding her head in a book all day. What about real life? Have a conversation. I'm right there.

DELL doesn't look up from her magazine.

BIRDY: How was Poe at the doctor?

DELL: Fine.

BIRDY: He didn't mind it?

DELL: No.

BIRDY: Did they let him keep the cast?

DELL: No.

BIRDY: We kept yours. They weren't plastic though then. They made them of real plaster then. That's why they called them plaster casts. You had all those signatures on it. Where is that I wonder?

DELL: Don't know.

BIRDY: Probably in the basement.

DELL: Probably.

BIRDY: He's like you, you were a climber too.

DELL: Yeah.

BIRDY: Did you get him a treat?

DELL: Yeah.

BIRDY: Ice cream.

DELL: He can't have ice cream.

BIRDY: I mean frozen yogourt or whatever they do now.

DELL: Yeah.

BIRDY: So you're not talking to me at all?

DELL: I'm talking.

BIRDY: No you're not.

DELL: I'm answering your questions.

BIRDY: But you're not talking *to* me.

DELL: What would you like me to talk to you about, Mom? Do you want me to talk about my day? Do you want me to talk about my other son who you don't even mention anymore? Do you want me to talk about how the school called and my other son won't answer his teachers if they don't call him Alice? Do you want me to talk about how I'm supposed to deal with that? Do you want me to talk about how it's all my fault and I'm supposed to know what to do about it because I'm his mother and I should just magically know? Or about how I'm just supposed to do nothing about it and hope it all goes away if I make him watch war movies and read him stories about cowboys? Would you like me to talk about that?

BIRDY: You're making such a big thing about it, Dell.

DELL: Some teacher wants to talk to me.

BIRDY: Not tonight, Dell.

DELL: Good. Any more questions?

BIRDY: No.

DELL: Good.

    DELL rises to leave.

Aunt Maddy called.

BIRDY: Was she having a drink?

DELL: Probably.

DELL exits.

BIRDY: Good. Where's the phone and where's the rum?

SCENE 7

PATRICIA's sitting room.

DELL places a tea tray down. PATRICIA enters from off expecting to see BIRDY.

PATRICIA: How did you get in here?

DELL: Key?

PATRICIA: Leave or I'll call the police.

DELL: What, I broke in to make tea?

PATRICIA: I'm serious.

DELL: I'm Dell. Bernice's daughter.

PATRICIA: She said everyone calls her Birdy.

DELL: Well when I'm talking to her I call her Mom. But when I'm talking about her I call her Bernice because I know it would drive her crazy.

PATRICIA: Where's your mother?

DELL: You didn't get her message obviously.

PATRICIA: I had the phone turned off, I'm just getting up.

DELL: Yeah I could hear you up there. Are you going somewhere?

PATRICIA: Pardon me?

DELL: You look like you're going somewhere.

PATRICIA: Where's your mother?

DELL: Death in the family.

PATRICIA: I see. Well.

This is rather unusual I think.

DELL: She didn't want to leave you hanging.

PATRICIA: I'll be fine for today thank you very much.

DELL: Don't be mad at her, she left a message.

PATRICIA: I beg your pardon?

DELL: Don't be mad at me, I'm the one who showed up.

PATRICIA: I'll be fine for today thank you.

DELL: There's tea there.

The kids are in school and I have nothing to do.

I'll hang out for a few minutes and you can tell her I stayed for an hour okay?

DELL sits.

I noticed you didn't have coffee. That's good, you shouldn't be drinking coffee.

PATRICIA: I shouldn't be?

DELL: And Bernice mentioned you liked your white wine. You should probably switch to red for the inflammation.

PATRICIA: Your mother discusses my medical history with you?

DELL: Why not?

PATRICIA: I don't appreciate being the subject of other people's conversations.

DELL: Well everybody is, for everybody else. If we didn't have other people to talk about what would we talk about? The weather and television.

PATRICIA: Ideas perhaps?

DELL: Whatcha got?

PATRICIA: Pardon me?

DELL: Throw an idea at me.

After a moment.

Yeah I know, not much going on these days but the weather. Your tea's getting cold.

PATRICIA sits.

So how are things going with Bernice?

PATRICIA: Well she's been with me two days and now she's sent her daughter in her place so it's hard to say.

DELL: Can't blame her for a death in the family.

PATRICIA: No.

DELL: Look here's something you should know, she's a talker but the trick is you don't have to listen. She'd love it if people listened but it's not required. She's just giving off energy verbally. Just nod once in a while and she'll be fine.

After a moment.

PATRICIA: Actually I've read that white is better than red wine.

DELL: Red's good for inflammation. In moderation. But it's hard on the head.

PATRICIA: Yes.

DELL: And it's all hard on the liver.

After a moment.

PATRICIA: Your mother mentioned you had some knowledge of medical marijuana.

DELL: What? Yeah. Some.

PATRICIA: Does it work?

DELL: It works for me.

PATRICIA: What are you treating?

DELL: Life.

PATRICIA: I see.

DELL: I'm thinking about doing a course in alternative medicine type stuff. Open a clinic maybe. Out in the woods, off the grid. Just me and Poe and Alice.

PATRICIA: Poe and Alice?

DELL: My kids.

PATRICIA: Oh, your mother mentioned you had two boys.

DELL: Yeah. Poe and Wolfgang. But Wolfgang wants to be called Alice now. *Alice in Wonderland* maybe, I read it to him.

PATRICIA: Ah.

DELL: It's no big deal. Freaks Bernice out though. Freaks the school out too. Some of them. One of them especially.

PATRICIA: He'll only answer to Alice?

DELL: Yeah.

PATRICIA: Did he change his name after enrolment?

DELL: It's pretty new . . . Yeah.

PATRICIA: That's what creates the issue, had you enrolled him as Alice there would be no argument. The change after enrolment gives them some cause to object, but the objection would not be supported at the board level.

DELL: It seems a lot to get into.

PATRICIA: It's really a case of personality at this point.

DELL: A personality thing? So more like a phase?

PATRICIA: I mean with the school.

DELL: Right.

DELL rises. After a moment DELL approaches PATRICIA. She stands a few feet away.

You have kids?

PATRICIA: No.

DELL: I definitely get a kid vibe from you.

PATRICIA: I had my students.

DELL holds her hand out and scans the energy from PATRICIA's upper torso and chest.

Why do you do that?

DELL: Energy. This area. Physics.

PATRICIA: Oh.

DELL: Your students loved you.

PATRICIA shifts away in her chair.

PATRICIA: I really will be fine today. You can go.

DELL: Sure.

PATRICIA: Who died?

DELL: A cousin. They weren't that close but she's the one they call. Bernice loves a crisis.

PATRICIA: Was it the cousin with the dog?

DELL: The dog? I don't think he had a dog.

PATRICIA: Oh no, never mind. Your mother mentioned something about a cousin with a dog.

DELL: Oh yeah, Vivian probably. Nasty dog.

PATRICIA: She mentioned that yes.

DELL: She'd be thrilled you were listening.

DELL exits.

PATRICIA holds her hand over her chest, wondering if she can feel the energy too.

SCENE 8

PATRICIA's sitting room. One week later.

PATRICIA stands drinking a glass of red wine. When she moves she stumbles gently.

PATRICIA: You know what else I don't like? I don't like tentative people. No I shouldn't say that I don't like them. I prefer not to be in their company. There's something about tentative people. The deferrals, the apologies. "What would you like to do? Well what would you like to do? Whatever you'd like to do." I mean, these are people who spend the evening standing on a corner imagining a restaurant is going to choose them.

Someone's got to make a damn decision. That's how I got my reputation. They called me "The General."

She finishes off her wine.

Or, "I'm so sorry." "I'm soooo sorry." Oh shut up. Just be sorry or don't be sorry, what is soooo sorry? How much more than sorry? It's something that makes me . . . not like them.

"I'm sooooo sorry."

I mean that's not exactly "tentative." But it's . . . overdone. Be simple, be direct. Which isn't to say have no discretion. Be direct in discretion to the situation. But don't be tentative.

It's actually textbook passive aggression. It ends up becoming all about the tentative person. In their effort to defer, to please, to . . . I don't know, be polite? To be liked. This tentative sucks all the energy out of the experience.

Call me many things but never tentative.

BIRDY enters with a moving box and puts it down.

BIRDY: Look at you prattling away.

PATRICIA: I'm having an idea or two.

BIRDY takes the empty wine glass from PATRICIA.

BIRDY: Have some tea.

PATRICIA: I've had my tea.

(noting the box) Oh, we're not getting into that.

BIRDY: You gotta just go through them. You have that room upstairs filled with boxes.

PATRICIA: We'll just call it the box room.

BIRDY: *(looking in the box)* It looks like dishes.

PATRICIA: Let me see.

BIRDY holds up a plate.

It's china, that can stay.

BIRDY: And this.

BIRDY takes a small ceramic box out of some tissue.

PATRICIA: Toss it.

BIRDY: It's so pretty.

PATRICIA: Every box is full of pretty. Just put it in the recycling.

BIRDY: There's not a crack on it or anything.

PATRICIA: *(waving her hand at BIRDY)* Toss it out.

BIRDY: Let me see your hand.

PATRICIA shows the other hand.

PATRICIA: My hand's fine.

BIRDY: No, the other one.

PATRICIA: Oh it's just—

BIRDY: Let me see.

BIRDY inspects PATRICIA's hand.

That's all fluid.

PATRICIA: I guess.

PATRICIA winces at BIRDY's touch.

BIRDY: That hurts does it?

PATRICIA: When you push on it like that.

BIRDY begins gently massaging PATRICIA's hand as they speak.

BIRDY: Dell's got a friend who does beautiful massages. I mean one thing she wanted to do to me was what I'd call *out there*.

Just hold her hands over me type thing, not touching me but just holding her hand like that over me. It's real or whatever, she studied it in some school. I said no thanks, not for me. I was worried next thing there'd be a Ouija board.

Is that better?

PATRICIA: Yes.

BIRDY: Dell says it's better you're switching to red wine.

PATRICIA: It does the same trick.

BIRDY: But maybe that saying, less is more?

PATRICIA: It's all that works.

BIRDY: 'Cause you're not taking the pills.

PATRICIA: I don't like the pills.

BIRDY: I don't think you're supposed to like them.

PATRICIA: I'm feeling pretty good right now actually.

BIRDY: Because you're drunk.

PATRICIA: I will not be policed.

BIRDY: Policed?

PATRICIA: I will not be.

BIRDY: Policed?

PATRICIA: Yes.

BIRDY: Okay.

PATRICIA: Okay.

PATRICIA takes her hand away.

That's fine. Thank you.

After a moment.

BIRDY: Did your husband ever do that?

PATRICIA: My husband?

BIRDY: Give you a hand massage? Sean used to, and my feet too.

PATRICIA: Why is everything an excuse for a travelogue of your life?

A stunned silence.

After a moment BIRDY rises and picks up the box.

What will we do with the china then?

BIRDY: I'll put it back in the box room.

BIRDY exits.

PATRICIA sits in the silence of regret.

SCENE 9

BIRDY's living room. That evening.

DELL sits with textbooks and a notebook open before her. BIRDY arrives home and places a shopping bag on the sofa.

BIRDY: What's a travelogue exactly?

DELL: A travelogue?

BIRDY: A description of a trip?

DELL: Pretty much.

BIRDY: So a travelogue of your life would be a description of your life.

DELL: I would think.

BIRDY: And what's wrong with that? It would be the other I think would be worse. Not saying nothing ever? What kind of person is that? And not a picture anywhere. Not even of the husband. I can't imagine there's any kids. Imagine that as a mother.

DELL: She doesn't have kids.

BIRDY: Really?

DELL: Yeah.

BIRDY: How do you know?

DELL: She told me when I was over there.

BIRDY: She told you? How?

DELL: I asked her and she told me.

BIRDY: You asked her and she told you?

DELL: Yeah.

BIRDY: Well she didn't tell me.

DELL: Did you ask?

BIRDY: What did her husband do?

DELL: I didn't ask.

BIRDY: Apparently her nickname was "The General."

DELL: How do you know that?

BIRDY: She told me.

DELL: Well there, she's telling you things, you're getting along.

BIRDY: Speaking of getting, look what I got.

DELL: What?

BIRDY: In the bag.

DELL looks in the bag.

DELL: What is it?

DELL takes the ceramic box out of the bag.

BIRDY: Not a crack on it. She was going to throw it out.

DELL: You took it?

BIRDY: She was going to throw it out.

DELL: You can't just take things.

BIRDY: She was going to throw it out.

BIRDY admires the box.

It's pretty. Not a feeling about it. "I've got enough pretty," that's her feeling about it.

DELL: You don't know her feelings.

BIRDY: Is "policed" a real word?

DELL: Policed?

BIRDY: Yeah, policed.

DELL: Yeah. Police, policing, policed.

BIRDY: Oh yeah, policing.

DELL: Why? Who's talking about policing?

BIRDY: Her. She won't have me policing her drinking.

DELL: You can't be bossy about it.

BIRDY: Her hands are starting to swell up like you wouldn't believe. And let's not talk about a fall.

BIRDY places the box down and admires it.

DELL: If you want to say hi Poe's out back and Alice is in his room.

BIRDY: Stop that.

DELL: Mom—

BIRDY: Just stop it. That's ridiculous. It's one thing to call him some other name in front of him so he'll even look at you but you don't have to be doing it when he's not in the room.

That's crossing the line.

DELL: Who makes the line? You.

BIRDY: You're making it worse.

DELL: Good night.

DELL takes her books and leaves.

SCENE 10

PATRICIA's sitting room. Two weeks later.

BIRDY and PATRICIA are returning from an excursion. We hear them entering from off.

PATRICIA: I should have moved to Arizona.

BIRDY: Here let me take your arm.

PATRICIA: Leave me now, you'll knock me over.

PATRICIA is wearing a buttoned trench coat.

BIRDY: What's in Arizona?

PATRICIA: Not this weather.

BIRDY: I'm sure it rains in Arizona too.

PATRICIA: Not for a month at a time.

BIRDY: It does that everywhere now apparently. Oh shit, we forgot to go to the bank.

PATRICIA: Oh damn.

BIRDY: I'll drop in on my way home.

PATRICIA: Are you going now?

BIRDY: I was going to. Do you need something?

PATRICIA: I don't know.

BIRDY: Tea?

PATRICIA: I don't know.

> PATRICIA *starts unbuttoning her coat, her fingers giving her a great deal of difficulty.* BIRDY *moves to help* PATRICIA, *but* PATRICIA *waves her away.*

That was a waste of an afternoon.

BIRDY: No it wasn't, we got those new pain pills. And I like that Dr. Hannah.

PATRICIA: I don't like him.

BIRDY: I do. He really talks to you when he talks to you. Not like some doctors, blah blah blah, never looking you in the eye, let's get on with it, here's your pills I'm going golfing.

PATRICIA: Hannah doesn't strike me as a golfer.

BIRDY: Or sailing or whatever they do doctors. I mean apparently Hannah does all that stuff too but he'll at least have a conversation.

PATRICIA: I'm not looking for conversation from my doctor.

> BIRDY *takes a bottle of pills from her pocket.*

BIRDY: You'll want one of these now.

PATRICIA: I took one in the car.

BIRDY: No you said you were going to and I said wait till you got home so you could have it with water.

PATRICIA: *(re: pill bottle)* Give me that here.

BIRDY: Let me read it first.

PATRICIA: With food, without food, one in the morning, two at night, what difference does it make. No I won't operate heavy machinery.

BIRDY: Oh.

PATRICIA: What?

BIRDY: You can't drink on them.

PATRICIA: At all?

BIRDY: Nope.

PATRICIA: Well a glass of wine's not going to make a difference.

BIRDY: At all.

PATRICIA: Oh God. Will I have nothing left? Not even a glass of wine. What's the point? I mean really. Staving off the inevitable. Time to spend with nothing to spend it on.

BIRDY: Well it could be worse—you could have no time to spend.

PATRICIA: A useless surplus.

BIRDY: I say though at the end of the day Dr. Hannah's doing everything he can.

PATRICIA: Doctors are useless. You ask for an encyclopedia and they hand you a telephone book.

BIRDY: A telephone book?

PATRICIA: Just as useful.

BIRDY: Well a telephone book is useful if you're looking for a number.

PATRICIA: I don't want a number. I want a solution.

BIRDY: Well I don't know, I think Dr. Hannah's nice.

PATRICIA: I don't want nice. This positivity, this sunniness. It's not sunny all the time, it's not sunny when it rains. And yes it's good for the farmers and the ducks but it's still raining. Someone told them that, stay on the sunny side of the street, look for the silver lining, people are good, life is precious. Someone told them that and they believed them.

After a moment.

BIRDY: I believe them.

PATRICIA: Good for you.

After a moment.

BIRDY: It's hard to lose your husband.

PATRICIA: What do you know about it.

BIRDY: I'm saying I can imagine how you feel.

PATRICIA: We're not friends you and I.

After a moment.

BIRDY: I never said we were.

After a moment.

PATRICIA: If you're going to the bank you better go.

BIRDY: I think I might just go home.

PATRICIA: Fine.

BIRDY: Fine.

BIRDY leaves.

SCENE 11

BIRDY's living room. That evening.

BIRDY sits on the sofa speaking off to DELL.

BIRDY: I mean it's pretty funny though, I'll just say. All my life the one thing that people said is that I'm good with people. That I make people comfortable. Even a room of strangers. I can walk into a room full of strangers and not feel a bit about it, have a chat with everyone, have a laugh with anyone pretty much. *Her* though. *Mrs. Branch.* She'd be *lucky* I'd be her friend. And I am good with people. That's one of my for sure good points. Always the kind of thing people went out of their way to come back later and tell me.

The phone rings off.

(re: phone) If that's Maddy get me a rum.

The phone is answered off.

Sean always said it was chemistry. That I have good chemistry with people. So I guess what we've got here is a chemistry problem. I never liked chemistry problems.

DELL appears with the phone.

DELL: It's Patricia.

BIRDY: Who? I don't know any Patricia. I only know Mrs. Branch. Mrs. Branch who I used to work for but do not any more.

BIRDY leaves.

Left with the phone DELL *considers her options with some dread. Finally:*

DELL: *(into phone)* Hey what's up?

End of Act One.

ACT TWO
SCENE 12

PATRICIA's sitting room. That night.

PATRICIA sits in the more formal, firmer chair. A tray of medications sits on the side table.

PATRICIA: *(speaking off)* Thank you for coming. I just had a bit of a panic not being able to get any of the pill bottles open. I suppose I might have gone next door to ask the neighbours but that's not how it's done in the city. One doesn't just go knocking on a door. One doesn't answer the door if one doesn't know who's there. I guess I should get to know my neighbours. I didn't realize you lived so close by.

DELL enters with a glass of water.

DELL: Here you go.

PATRICIA: Thank you.

DELL: *(taking water)* I told you that chair would be better for your back.

PATRICIA: Yes. Thank you.

DELL: You need more support.

PATRICIA: Yes.

I didn't realize that you lived so nearby. Your mother never mentioned it. I didn't notice it on her resumé. The address.

DELL: Her resumé. She never had to have a resumé before.

PATRICIA: I can be unnecessarily formal at times.

DELL: Yeah well Bernice can be unnecessarily informal.

PATRICIA: Thank you for coming. I thought your mother might.

DELL: Not tonight.

PATRICIA: It was just a bit of a panic. I couldn't open the bottle because my hands were so stiff and I had to take the pill to get rid of the stiffness.

DELL is looking through PATRICIA's medications on the side table.

DELL: How's the pain?

PATRICIA: Up and down. Mostly up.

DELL: *(re: a pill bottle)* These are strong.

PATRICIA: The painkillers? I don't take those. They make me . . . fuzzy and strange.

DELL: So what are you doing for pain?

PATRICIA: I switched to red wine.

DELL: Yeah, I noticed an empty bottle in the kitchen.

PATRICIA: That may have had something to do with my panic.

DELL: The bottle of wine?

PATRICIA: That I couldn't get the second bottle opened. It helps.

Or it helps me not think about it.

DELL: This might help more.

>*DELL takes out a small bag of marijuana.*

PATRICIA: Oh. No, I don't think so.

DELL: Maybe try it.

You'll be my first patient.

PATRICIA: I tried it once years ago. It made me all up in my head.

DELL: Try it baked. A cookie, bread, on toast.

PATRICIA: On toast?

DELL: Sprinkle it on bread and toast it in the oven.

PATRICIA: I can't imagine it would be very tasty.

DELL: Add some honey.

It'll keep you out of your head more.

>*DELL puts the package on the table beside PATRICIA.*

Hang on to it.

PATRICIA: No no.

DELL: Or throw it out. Or hang on to it.

PATRICIA: For an emergency?

DELL: For a nice afternoon.

After a moment.

PATRICIA: In regards to your mother . . .

DELL: She doesn't have a filter.

PATRICIA: Did she tell you what happened?

DELL: Just that you didn't want to be her friend.

PATRICIA: That's not what I said.

DELL: That's what she heard.

PATRICIA: I suppose she thinks I'm a terrible person.

DELL: Are you?

PATRICIA: I hope not.

DELL: Well I am.

PATRICIA: You are? . . .

DELL: A terrible person.

PATRICIA: You are?

DELL: Terrible at it. At being a person. It seems like to be a person it has to all about me. My beliefs, my opinions, my outrage. Everybody's so outraged about everything. So righteously outraged. It's all about politics. Religion. War.

PATRICIA: Well, those are just motivations, impulses. Impulses that lead us to motivation. A person is more than their motivations.

DELL: A *human* maybe. That's something else. But a *person*?

PATRICIA: And the difference between a person and a human?

DELL: Politics. And religion. And war.

PATRICIA: Some people say that religion and war are the same thing.

DELL: All politics.

PATRICIA: Indeed.

DELL: Bernice has trouble with the person thing too, but she's a good human.

PATRICIA: Perhaps a filter is part of personhood.

DELL: I'll have a talk with her.

    DELL moves to leave.

PATRICIA: How are your boys?

DELL: Poe wants to play hockey. He's still too young. But I see a lot of hours in a rink ahead.

PATRICIA: And Alice? Is he still Alice?

DELL: Yeah. And I let him be. Is that bad?

PATRICIA: I'm no expert.

DELL: You were a teacher.

PATRICIA: At the end I was more an administrator. When I was teaching it was a few years ago. We never came up against these kinds of problems.

DELL: You know, I'm not even sure it's a problem. It's not a problem for Alice. He just goes merrily along. I mean there's bad stuff going on around him but none of it sticks to him.

It's like he's made of love.

PATRICIA: Made of love.

DELL: One of the teachers called and said I needed to "play by the rules" or they'd be talking about expelling him.

PATRICIA: They can't do that.

DELL: Maybe if we were in the city. Or in the woods.

PATRICIA: What are your mother's thoughts?

DELL: I don't know. She won't talk about it.

PATRICIA: What do you imagine?

DELL: It's the kind of thing she would have let my father handle and just gone along with him.

PATRICIA: And how would your father have handled it?

DELL: Not well.

> DELL *moves to leave.*

If you're fine now I'll head out.

PATRICIA: I've enjoyed our chat.

DELL: Yes.

Toast and honey.

DELL exits.

PATRICIA examines the bag of marijuana.

SCENE 13

BIRDY's living room. A little later.

DELL has just arrived back from PATRICIA's.

BIRDY: So you handled the big panic did you?

DELL: She just needed some help.

BIRDY: Oh yeah?

DELL: She's a very nice lady.

BIRDY: Is she?

DELL: Yes she is.

BIRDY: Yes sure, take her side, like you would.

DELL: Like I would?

BIRDY: Any side against me is the side you'll be on.

DELL: There are no sides. Why are there always sides for you?

BIRDY: She's rude to me.

DELL: How is she rude?

BIRDY: Telling me to shut up.

DELL: She told you to shut up?

BIRDY: More or less.

DELL: What did you say to make her more or less tell you to shut up?

BIRDY: I was just trying to have a chat, that's all.

DELL: You don't have a chat, you have an inquisition.

BIRDY: You weren't there.

DELL: And you're not there to chat, you're there to work.

BIRDY: Oh yes, she'd have me in a uniform with my head down never saying a word.

DELL: Well if that's what she wants you to do that's what you do.

BIRDY: Why should I?

DELL: What were you chatting about?

BIRDY: About nothing, just chat.

DELL: What was it she didn't want to chat about?

BIRDY: I don't know, Sean I guess, her husband.

DELL: Maybe she doesn't want to talk about her husband.

BIRDY: It's just a way to be pleasant with someone. It was just a pleasant conversation.

DELL: Maybe a pleasant conversation for you isn't a pleasant conversation for her.

BIRDY: She's rude.

DELL: You're nosy.

BIRDY: You watch yourself. You weren't there.

Nosy?

Honest to God.

DELL: You want to have a pleasant conversation with her talk about Alice.

BIRDY: Oh stop that.

DELL: You have such a problem with it maybe you need to talk about it to someone.

BIRDY: Oh for God's sake Dell it's not real.

DELL: It's very real Mom.

BIRDY: Because you're making it real!

After a moment.

He's just a kid. So what, he wants something. It's like people bringing their kids into a restaurant and giving them a menu and asking them what they want. You don't ask a kid what they want when they've got a hundred choices. Just get them the chicken fingers and be done with it.

DELL: It's more complicated than chicken fingers.

BIRDY: Complicated? It's not complicated it's kids.

DELL: Kids aren't complicated? I wasn't complicated.

BIRDY: No you weren't, you did what you were told. Until you got old enough to do just what you wanted.

How can you think those boys don't need a father?

DELL: They don't.

BIRDY: And maybe that's the problem we're looking at right there.

DELL: Meaning what?

BIRDY: These things don't just happen out of nothing, Dell. Somebody's at fault somewhere.

DELL: Alice is nobody's fault.

BIRDY: His name isn't Alice.

DELL: Not as far as he's concerned.

BIRDY: Oh my God, what did I do to deserve this?

DELL: Here's something I want you to think about for a minute, Bernice. It's not about you.

BIRDY: Then leave me out of it.

BIRDY exits. DELL is left alone and frustrated.

SCENE 14

PATRICIA's sitting room. The next morning.

BIRDY stands stiffly. Her jacket on, her purse on her shoulder.

BIRDY: I don't know what you and Dell talked about last night but the word she brought home was that I should come in today. I don't know exactly what for but here I am.

PATRICIA enters with tea on a tray. She struggles a bit but manages.

Give me that.

PATRICIA: I'm fine.

BIRDY: Come on now.

PATRICIA: I'm fine.

PATRICIA places the tea on the table.

See?

PATRICIA sits with some difficulty in the more formal chair.

Have tea with me.

BIRDY: Have tea?

PATRICIA: Have tea. Sit.

BIRDY regards PATRICIA's comfortable chair.

Sit.

With some trepidation BIRDY *sits.*

BIRDY: You're walking good today.

PATRICIA: I spoke harshly to you and I want to say I'm sorry.

BIRDY: Yeah well—

PATRICIA: I want to apologize.

After a moment.

BIRDY: I wasn't being nosy. I'm just having a chat, that's all. I'm not saying we have to be friends.

PATRICIA: You have a lot of friends?

BIRDY: I don't know.

Not like a lot. I mean I know everybody but not so much friends. My sister Maddy. A couple of girls I went to school with.

PATRICIA: Your husband was your friend?

BIRDY: Yes.

After a moment.

PATRICIA: My husband liked strawberry ice cream.

BIRDY: Oh.

After a moment.

Are you hungry?

Can I get you something to eat?

PATRICIA: Hm?

BIRDY: You want a bite to eat?

PATRICIA: No I'm fine thank you. I had some toast earlier.

BIRDY: Just toast?

PATRICIA: And honey.

Honey.

Did your husband call you honey?

After a moment.

BIRDY: Sometimes.

He always made fun of himself when he did. Almost like he did it by accident.

PATRICIA: That's nice.

After a moment.

"Chat." That's an interesting word, isn't it? Chat. It sounds just like what it is. Chat chat chat.

BIRDY: It's just a way to make people feel comfortable. But maybe you're not comfortable feeling comfortable.

Maybe that's what the wine's for.

PATRICIA: Perhaps.

BIRDY: What do you think about that?

PATRICIA: It's entirely possible.

BIRDY: At least you didn't do your "very good."

PATRICIA: My "very good"?

BIRDY: It's something you do when you want me to shut up.

PATRICIA: I suppose it's just a way to say let's move on.

BIRDY: Why do you get to be the one to say it's time to move on?

PATRICIA: Yes.

Good point. Yes.

Indeed.

BIRDY: *(imitating PATRICIA)* "Very good!"

PATRICIA: Oh. Yes. Do that again.

BIRDY: "Very good!"

PATRICIA: Very good.

> *This cracks PATRICIA up. She laughs for some time.*

BIRDY: Are you okay?

> *PATRICIA pours tea for BIRDY.*

PATRICIA: Yes I am.

I like your daughter. I like Dell. You raised her well.

BIRDY: I don't know about that.

PATRICIA shakily hands BIRDY her tea.

Thank you.

After a moment.

PATRICIA: I like Schubert.

BIRDY: I could get you some.

PATRICIA: You could get me some?

BIRDY: Dell gets it for the kids. No dairy.

PATRICIA: Oh did I say sherbet? I mean Schubert, the composer.

BIRDY: Oh right, well, yeah. I don't know about that.

PATRICIA: There's a concert on Saturday afternoon in the city. Schubert sonatas for piano.

BIRDY: Oh yeah.

PATRICIA: I'll often do that on Saturdays. Head in to the city. Sometimes a concert, or the theatre if there's a matinee, sometimes an art gallery.

Perhaps you'd like to come along.

BIRDY: To an art gallery?

PATRICIA: To the concert on Saturday.

BIRDY: I could drive you in.

PATRICIA: Perhaps you'd join me.

BIRDY: To see the concert?

PATRICIA: Yes.

BIRDY: I suppose I could.

Might be something different.

PATRICIA: Very good.

> PATRICIA *laughs.* BIRDY *laughs.*

How's the tea?

BIRDY: Nice.

PATRICIA: A nice afternoon.

> *After a moment.*

He died penniless.

BIRDY: Your husband?

PATRICIA: No no. Schubert. My husband penniless? Hardly. Money was his all.

BIRDY: But he liked strawberry ice cream.

PATRICIA: Yes. And that was pretty much his only soft spot.

BIRDY: Was he bad to you?

PATRICIA: No.

Withholding. Stubborn.

I always wanted children and I thought he'd change his mind. But he was not a man to change his mind. He was a stubborn bugger. So I said to hell with him and I went to school and became a teacher. He was mortified. No one in the family had actually worked before.

BIRDY: Nobody worked?

PATRICIA: I don't miss him. I feel like I should but I don't.

BIRDY: I'm sure lots of people feel that way.

PATRICIA: And I had my children in my students, but you know what I missed? Being a grandmother. An indulgent grandmother. A proud grandmother.

Would you say you were a proud grandmother?

BIRDY: Would I say . . . ? Yes, of course. Of course I would.

> *BIRDY rises, taking off her coat, and removes the tea tray. She exits talking.*

And now let's see about getting your pills put in something easier to open.

(off) Those little plastic boxes, you know, you get them at the drugstore— Monday, Tuesday, Wednesday. My aunt uses them. She doesn't bother with the days though, well at this point she doesn't know one day from the other. I just let her believe it's whatever day she wants it to be.

> *PATRICIA watches sadly off after BIRDY.*

SCENE 15

BIRDY's house. Saturday afternoon.

DELL sits waiting, holding a pair of earrings. BIRDY speaks from off.

BIRDY: *(off)* Oh my God I don't want to go to this damn concert.

DELL: Sure you do.

BIRDY enters more formally dressed than we have seen her. She takes the earrings from DELL and starts putting them on.

BIRDY: All those types who go to those concerts. Golfers.

DELL: Golfers?

BIRDY: Who goes to those concerts?

DELL: Lots of people.

BIRDY: And what is it anyway, what kind of music?

DELL: Schubert is . . . they call it Romantic.

BIRDY: Romantic?

DELL: It's a style. It's pretty. It's very popular.

BIRDY: It's not that popular I never heard of it. I heard of Beethoven.

DELL: It's like Beethoven.

BIRDY: I don't want to go. I'll drive her in and wait in the car.

DELL: No you won't. She's trying to be nice.

BIRDY: I know I know.

I can't get these damn earrings in, I think the holes grew over.

DELL: Come here.

BIRDY: I can get it.

Why is it that when people are trying to be nice they make you do things you don't want to do? When I'm trying to be nice I just bring cookies.

I can't find the damn holes.

DELL: Here.

> *DELL helps BIRDY with her earrings.*

You didn't take the backs off.

BIRDY: I haven't worn them in years. Ever since you wore one in your nose.

DELL: Once. I'm sorry.

BIRDY: And I've got to drive.

DELL: You're taking the car?

BIRDY: Oh no no, we've got to take her car. I don't like driving that big tank.

DELL: I'm going to take your car if that's all right.

BIRDY: What's wrong with the truck?

DELL: It's out of gas.

BIRDY: God Dell, they're not like lighters. You don't just throw them away when they're out of fluid.

DELL: The Civic gets better mileage.

BIRDY: Fine fine take the car. To go where?

DELL: Rawdon.

BIRDY: Who's in Rawdon?

DELL: I was talking to some people online. A couple who have a kid like Alice.

BIRDY: Like what?

DELL: So they can meet.

BIRDY: What?

DELL: Stay still.

BIRDY: No forget the damn earrings, what are you talking about?

DELL: I talked to the mother, on the phone, she has a seven-year-old boy who's decided he's a girl.

BIRDY: What? A girl? Decided? Kids aren't supposed to be deciding anything.

DELL: Or realized, how about that.

BIRDY: What are you saying? No. It's not right.

DELL: Alice wants to go.

BIRDY: Alice wants—? The kid wants? Kids want all kinds of things they don't get them. Everybody wants all kinds of things. I want all kinds of things.

DELL: Like what?

BIRDY: Like what?

DELL: What do you want?

BIRDY: I want . . . I want . . . Oh for God's sake, I don't know—I want your father back.

DELL: Well you can't have that. What do you want that you might be able to have?

BIRDY: Oh my God, I don't know.

DELL: Alice does.

BIRDY: I want everything to go back to how it was.

After a moment.

DELL: He'll only go to the girl's bathroom now at school. They say they can expel him.

BIRDY: Oh my God . . .

DELL: I don't know what to do.

I'm going to go and meet these people. I need some support.

After a moment.

Come here.

DELL finishes putting in BIRDY's earring.

BIRDY feels her earrings.

BIRDY: You got them? Good. Thank you.

DELL leaves.

We hear the beginning of the first section of Schubert's Moments Musicaux #2 in A Flat.

SCENE 16

Music continues.

The concert hall.

PATRICIA *listens to the Schubert. She is joined by* BIRDY. *We watch their faces side by side as they are watching the concert.*

As the section approaches its ending PATRICIA *steps away and* BIRDY *listens alone.*

SCENE 17

PATRICIA's sitting room. Later that day.

They have just arrived home from the concert. PATRICIA *puts her things away and sits.* BIRDY *is off preparing tea.*

PATRICIA: *(off to* BIRDY*)* You haven't said anything about the concert.

After a moment.

(off to BIRDY*)* You haven't said anything about the concert.

BIRDY: *(off)* I said it was good.

PATRICIA: *(off to* BIRDY*)* Why?

After a moment.

Why was it good?

BIRDY *enters wiping her hands.*

Why was it good?

BIRDY: Why? You know, it was good. I don't know what to say.

PATRICIA: What about the playing? Did you like the playing?

BIRDY: It was beautiful.

PATRICIA: Beautiful?

BIRDY: Beautiful playing. Beautiful music.

She was really good. I was surprised it was a woman.

PATRICIA: Why?

BIRDY: I don't know, I just thought it would be a man.

PATRICIA: What else surprised you?

BIRDY: I was surprised it was just a piano. I thought it would be like an orchestra or whatever.

PATRICIA: Where you disappointed it was just a piano?

BIRDY: No no no. Just surprised. She was really good.

BIRDY moves to leave; she stops.

And the people, that surprised me.

PATRICIA: That there were so many?

BIRDY: No that they were just . . . I was the most dressed up person there. Did you see that one guy eating his lunch?

PATRICIA: Yes.

BIRDY: Are they allowed to do that?

PATRICIA: It's discouraged.

BIRDY: Everybody was pretty regular.

PATRICIA: It was made for regular people. It used to be the music of the people at one time.

BIRDY: Before radio and all that you mean? Before singing?

PATRICIA: I think there was always singing.

BIRDY: Right. Opera and that. Before songs.

PATRICIA: Would you listen to it again?

BIRDY: I'm more used to songs.

PATRICIA: Right.

BIRDY moves to leave; she stops.

BIRDY: It had two different kind of feelings at the same time.

PATRICIA: What feelings?

BIRDY: It was really beautiful but it was also really sad.

PATRICIA: That's a good way to describe it.

BIRDY: To me something beautiful feels like it should be happy.

PATRICIA: There can be sadness in beauty, and true beauty in sadness.

BIRDY: Like it makes you want to cry but you didn't know why.

PATRICIA: Maybe because it was so beautiful.

BIRDY: Maybe,

PATRICIA: Sad and beautiful. That makes sense. Nothing really is just one thing, is it?

After a moment.

How are your grandchildren?

BIRDY: Good.

I'm not sure I plugged in that kettle.

BIRDY moves to leave. PATRICIA rises.

PATRICIA: I'll check it. You're not working today; we're just having a visit.

PATRICIA moves off to the kitchen.

BIRDY: Can we not talk about my grandchildren?

PATRICIA: We can talk about whatever you want.

BIRDY: If that's all right.

PATRICIA: Of course. We can talk about the music.

PATRICIA moves off into the kitchen.

BIRDY: *(off to PATRICIA)* I don't know why I said that. We can talk about the kids sure. But just kids today, you know? It's all so different. It's just all so . . . Yes the music, that's a good thing to talk about, let's talk about the music.

SCENE 18

BIRDY's living room. The next afternoon.

DELL and PATRICIA stand. PATRICIA is less steady on her feet than we have seen her.

DELL: Can I get you something? A glass of water?

PATRICIA: No I'm fine.

DELL: My mom's not here.

PATRICIA: Yes I know, she's running some errands for me.

I wanted to talk to you. And I wanted a bit of a walk. I haven't had a walk in a while. It's so close. Though it took me the better part of an hour.

DELL: Have a seat.

PATRICIA: I better not. Getting up is harder than standing.

DELL: I'll help you up.

PATRICIA: Well first you'll have to help me down.

DELL assists PATRICIA to sit. PATRICIA notices her ceramic box proudly displayed.

Oh, look at that.

DELL: Oh. Yeah.

Mom said you didn't want it.

PATRICIA: Oh no, yes, that's fine.

DELL: I mean if it's something special—

PATRICIA: It was a wedding gift.

DELL: To you?

PATRICIA: Um hm. Birdy found it in a packing box. I made it clear I didn't want it. I'm glad it's getting some use.

DELL: She doesn't use it. She just stares at it.

PATRICIA: Perhaps it has a secret to tell her?

DELL: A secret?

PATRICIA: I managed to locate the teacher.

DELL: The teacher?

PATRICIA: It's always the way. It doesn't take too many phone calls to find someone who knows someone who knows the teacher in question.

DELL: The teacher in question?

PATRICIA: In this case, the teacher who's giving you difficulty. The one who called and said you had to play by her rules.

DELL: You talked to her?

PATRICIA: No, in this case that would be imprudent.

PATRICIA hands DELL a note.

Call this man. He's on the school board. Tell him you were given his number by the woman who spoke with Deborah.

DELL: Who's Deborah?

PATRICIA: She teaches in the area. She seems very nice.

He'll be more than happy to discuss a solution. Her behaviour is very much outside policy.

DELL: How do you mean?

PATRICIA: You now hold the power. He'll explain. A solution will be reached.

DELL: Wow.

Thank you.

PATRICIA: There's no reason Alice shouldn't be in school. It's your right as a taxpayer. You should know your rights.

DELL: Thank you.

Mom thinks it's a phase.

PATRICIA: That may be, but whatever it is it's happening.

DELL: Sometimes I think it would be easier if we went off to the woods. On our own.

PATRICIA: You don't want to do that. We people need humans like you.

After a moment.

My students did love me. You were right about that. That's something I knew and I think I might have forgotten it. Thank you for reminding me.

After a moment.

I tried your toast.

DELL: You did?

PATRICIA: It does rather make for a nice afternoon.

DELL: Well, as your practitioner . . . If you ever need more? . . .

PATRICIA: Well . . . since I'm here . . .

DELL: I have some plants growing in the backyard. Would you like to see?

PATRICIA: I think I might indeed.

DELL helps PATRICIA up and leads her off. As they exit:

I'm intrigued to see the source of all this pleasantness.

DELL: You'd think it was a weed if you didn't know.

PATRICIA: Hence the slang "weed."

DELL: Yeah I guess.

PATRICIA: How does one go about getting a licence for this weed?

SCENE 19

PATRICIA's sitting room. That evening.

PATRICIA enters with her "honey toast" on a plate and settles in. She's about to have a bite as BIRDY bursts in.

BIRDY: Okay we're going to have a talk about this.

PATRICIA: Good God, you scared the life out of me!

BIRDY: We're going to talk about this right now.

PATRICIA: What?

BIRDY: What do you think you're doing?

PATRICIA: I'm just having some toast.

BIRDY: Dell says you were by the house today.

PATRICIA: Yes.

BIRDY: I don't appreciate, okay, I don't appreciate you getting involved in all this business.

PATRICIA: I'm going to get a licence.

BIRDY: A licence?

PATRICIA: I'm going to talk to Dr. Hannah and get a permit.

BIRDY: For what?

PATRICIA: The marijuana.

BIRDY: Oh my God. Has she got you on that?

PATRICIA: I just put it on toast.

BIRDY: So that's why all of a sudden we're running a toast factory here.

PATRICIA: I'm going to get a permit.

BIRDY: I don't care about your permit or your stupid pot. Stay out of the business with the boy.

PATRICIA: With Alice?

BIRDY: Don't start that too.

PATRICIA: I'm trying to help.

BIRDY: Well you're not helping.

Did you hook her up with those people on the computer?

PATRICIA: Which people?

BIRDY: The people with the kid.

PATRICIA: I don't know what you mean.

BIRDY: You're all making it worse by paying attention to it. Just let it be.

PATRICIA: Haven't you already tried that?

BIRDY: Then let it be longer.

PATRICIA: Maybe it's a phase.

BIRDY: That's what I'm saying, it's a phase!

PATRICIA: Maybe it is, but whatever it is it has to be handled gently, calmly.

BIRDY: Well there's nothing calm about all this. You know what that fella you told her to call said to do? Contact the newspaper. Call the TV. God almighty. This is what kids do, they do this stuff to try to get attention.

PATRICIA: Is Alice not getting enough attention?

BIRDY: Stop calling him that! Oh God!

PATRICIA: Why does it bother you so much, Birdy?

BIRDY: Because I don't know what to do!

After a moment.

Look, in the city people get up to whatever they get up to and there's so many people nobody notices, or nobody cares. People notice here. They care. It's different in the city.

PATRICIA: I don't think it's any different anywhere. Or it's all different. It's all just more and more different.

BIRDY: That's the toast talking.

After a moment.

PATRICIA: Something is broken. But Alice isn't. Something is. Some idea of yours. Throw it out.

BIRDY: Like it's that easy.

PATRICIA: Why is it supposed to be easy?

BIRDY: Can't *anything* be easy?

PATRICIA: Not really, no.

After a moment.

BIRDY: It doesn't seem to bother Dell at all.

PATRICIA: It does.

BIRDY: What am I supposed to say when people ask?

PATRICIA: You don't have to say anything.

BIRDY: Oh come on. Around here? I'll have to say something. What? "This is my grandson Alice?"

PATRICIA: Just say you're a proud grandmother.

After a moment.

Would you like some toast?

BIRDY: No I would not.

BIRDY moves to leave.

PATRICIA: I'm sorry this is so difficult for you.

BIRDY: Yeah. Thanks.

PATRICIA: It's just a name.

BIRDY: For now.

BIRDY leaves.

SCENE 20

BIRDY's living room. Later that evening.

DELL sits working on a paper. BIRDY enters.

DELL: Where did you go?

BIRDY: Are the kids in bed?

DELL: I just tucked them in, you want to say good night?

BIRDY: Gimme some of that stuff.

DELL: What stuff?

BIRDY: That pot.

DELL: No.

BIRDY: Why not?

DELL: You don't need it.

BIRDY: And you do?

DELL: I haven't for a while.

BIRDY: You're giving it to her.

DELL: She told you?

BIRDY: It's pretty clear to see. She didn't start inviting me to concerts without smoking something.

DELL: I'm her practitioner.

BIRDY: Her practitioner?

DELL: Yes.

BIRDY: Look at you. You'll be golfing next.

DELL: It's helping her. Her mood. The swelling even.

BIRDY: Gimme some.

DELL: No.

BIRDY: Why not?

DELL: I've seen you on it.

BIRDY: You have not.

DELL: Yes. You and Dad one time.

BIRDY: When?

DELL: I was around ten. You had a party here and everybody left but you and Dad and Maddy, and I was up on the stairs.

BIRDY: Spying.

DELL: Of course. I was ten.

BIRDY: Well that would have been Maddy for sure.

DELL: It was you too. I saw you. You couldn't stop laughing. It just made you silly.

BIRDY: Maybe.

After a moment.

Your father, he could make me laugh.

I know you had your disagreements. And so did I with him, more than you saw. But he could make me laugh. And he could listen. See that's the thing, he'd just listen and listen.

DELL: He wasn't much for conversation.

BIRDY: And he'd let me go on and on. And at the end of it, he'd let me get right to the end of it and he'd say "It'll be all right." And not just for something to say. Like he meant it. Like he knew it.

You know what else he used to say? "You gotta leave room for other people to talk."

DELL touches her mother.

DELL: It'll be all right.

BIRDY: It's not fair.

DELL: About Dad?

BIRDY: About Alice.

SCENE 21

PATRICIA's sitting room. One month later.

A small gift box and a tiny gift box sit on the table. PATRICIA *and* DELL *are sitting. A walker now stands beside* PATRICIA.

BIRDY enters with cake on two plates.

BIRDY: You didn't make a wish when you blew out the candles.

PATRICIA: Yes I did. I wished the cake wasn't gluten-free.

BIRDY: *(re: DELL)* She can't have gluten. Were you surprised?

PATRICIA: No. Why would I be surprised? You've been talking about my birthday for the last month. Ever since you snooped through my things to find out when it was.

BIRDY: I didn't snoop. They told me at the bank.

PATRICIA: They told you?

BIRDY: It was right there on your information.

PATRICIA: They told you?

BIRDY: Asking isn't snooping.

BIRDY takes a bite of cake.

Oh brother.

PATRICIA: It is gluten-free I take it.

BIRDY: She can't have gluten.

PATRICIA: So much for wishing.

DELL: It's not so bad. I get them all the time for the kids. They don't know the difference.

PATRICIA: You don't allow the children gluten?

BIRDY: Alice gets a bad stomach from it.

Eat your cake.

PATRICIA: I'll have it later.

BIRDY: Take a bite. It's bad luck not to take a bite of your birthday cake.

PATRICIA: I took a bite. I miss gluten.

BIRDY: It's got a kind of wild taste doesn't it? Like moose.

DELL: Moose?

BIRDY: Moose compared to cow. You know how moose has that gamey taste.

PATRICIA: Ugh.

BIRDY: It's gamey, the cake. Not bad but like you can taste the farm in it.

PATRICIA: Just what I'm looking for in a cake.

BIRDY: Now open your presents.

PATRICIA: It really wasn't necessary.

BIRDY: It's just a couple of things.

PATRICIA: It really wasn't necessary.

BIRDY: Open mine.

BIRDY hands PATRICIA the small box.

PATRICIA: Thank you.

PATRICIA attempts to unwrap the box.

BIRDY: You can rip it if you want.

PATRICIA is having some trouble with her finger mobility.

PATRICIA: I'm having a bit of . . .

BIRDY: Here, I'll do it. Can I rip it?

PATRICIA: If you must.

BIRDY rips the paper off the box with pleasure. She takes out PATRICIA's ceramic box and hands it to her.

BIRDY: It's your box.

PATRICIA: Yes I can see that.

BIRDY: I didn't know it was from your wedding. You gotta hold on to that stuff. You can't just go tossing out stuff like that.

PATRICIA: May I offer it as a gift? Allow me to offer it to you as a gift.

PATRICIA hands BIRDY back the box.

BIRDY: That's not why I gave—

PATRICIA: It's a gift from me.

BIRDY: Thank you.

DELL hands PATRICIA the tiny box.

DELL: You don't have to open it now.

BIRDY: Oh I know what that is. A present from the pusher.

PATRICIA: My practitioner.

BIRDY: I guess you're going to have a nice afternoon now.

PATRICIA: It's already a nice afternoon.

BIRDY admires the ceramic box.

Turn it on.

BIRDY: Turn it on?

PATRICIA: Wind it up. On the bottom.

BIRDY looks.

BIRDY: There's nothing here.

DELL: Let me see.

DELL takes the box from BIRDY.

PATRICIA: You have to reach in and it pulls out.

DELL: Oh yeah.

BIRDY: Look at that!

DELL winds the box. We hear the tiny tune. It's the Schubert sonata.

It's so sad.

PATRICIA: And beautiful.

DELL: Yes.

BIRDY: Yes it is.

PATRICIA conducts the tiny orchestra as the light fades.

End.

Daniel MacIvor is one of Canada's most accomplished playwrights and performers. Winner of the prestigious Elinore and Lou Siminovitch Prize, the GLAAD Award, the Governor General's Literary Award and many others, Daniel's plays have been met with acclaim throughout North America.

First edition: March 2016
Printed and bound in Canada by Imprimerie Gauvin, Gatineau

Cover photos and headshot © Guntar Kravis

**PLAYWRIGHTS
CANADA PRESS**
202-269 Richmond St. W.
Toronto, ON
M5V 1X1

416.703.0013
info@playwrightscanada.com
www.playwrightscanada.com
@playcanpress

RECYCLED
Paper made from
recycled material
FSC® C100212
www.fsc.org